Jennie Carter

Jennie Carter

A Black Journalist of the Early West

Edited by Eric Gardner

University Press of Mississippi / *Jackson*

Margaret Walker Alexander Series
in African American Studies

www.upress.state.ms.us

The University Press of Mississippi is a member
of the Association of American University Presses.

Paperback Edition 2010

∞

Library of Congress Cataloging-in-Publication Data
Carter, Jennie, 1830 or 31–1881.
Jennie Carter : a Black journalist of the early West /
edited by Eric Gardner.—1st ed.
    p. cm.—(Margaret Walker Alexander series in
African American studies)
    Consists mainly of Carter's contributions to the
San Francisco Elevator and the Philadelphia-based
Christian recorder, from 1867 to 1881.
    Includes bibliographical references and index.
    ISBN-13: 978-1-934110-10-2 (cloth : alk. paper)
    ISBN-10: 1-934110-10-8 (cloth : alk. paper)
    1. African Americans—California—Social
conditions—19th century. 2. African Americans—
West (U.S.)—Social conditions—19th century
    3. West (U.S.)—Social conditions—19th century.
    4. West (U.S.)—Race realtions—History—19th
century. 5. California—Politics and government—
1850–1950. 6. United States—Politics and
government—1865–1877. 7. United States—Race
relations—History—19th century. 8. Carter, Jennie,
1830 or 31–1881—Correspondence. 9. African American
women journalists—California—Nevada County—
Correspondence. 10. Nevada County (Calif.)—
Biography. I. Gardner, Eric. II. Elevator
(San Francisco, Calif.) III. Christian recorder. IV. Title.
    E185.93.C2C385 2007
    070.92—dc22
    [B]   2007013714

British Library Cataloging-in-Publication Data available

Contents

Always Faithful

An Introduction to the Work and Life of Jennie Carter

In June 1867, a woman calling herself "Ann J. Trask" and claiming to live on "Mud Hill" in Nevada County, California, wrote to Philip A. Bell, one of the foremost African American journalists in the nation. At the time, Bell was editing the *Elevator*, a weekly San Francisco black newspaper he had founded two years earlier, and "Mrs. Trask" told him that she had "been a reader of your excellent paper for some time" and was grateful "for your efforts on behalf of our people." She noted, though, that, now that "our children and grand-children are readers, and to encourage reading," Bell should "have in each number a short story for them." She concluded her letter with the simple promise, "If you like the idea, and think my scribbling any account, I will write for you."[1]

In his next issue, Bell published that letter and an accompanying short narrative—the sentimental story of the death of Trask's beloved dog Nino during her New Orleans childhood. It was the first of over seventy pieces that the woman who initially called herself "Ann J. Trask" would publish in the *Elevator* over the next seven years. Though she occasionally shared poems, the vast majority of her work took the form of pithy essays and narratives that were often headed, simply, "Letter from Nevada County." Trask's contributions quickly moved beyond her plan of "writing for the children," and she "wound up writing for everybody" (16 August 1867 *Elevator*). The rich body of her work, collected for the first time in this volume, considers California and national politics, race and racism, women's rights and suffrage, temperance, morality, education, and a host of other issues—all from the point of view of an unabashedly strong African American woman.

Early on, "Mrs. Trask" added a second penname, one she would, in the end, use much more: "Semper Fidelis," Latin for "always faithful."[2] Bell clearly knew that "Ann J. Trask" and "Semper Fidelis" were pennames. Beyond consistently saying that he would not publish any contribution that carried a pseudonym unless he knew the author's identity, he went so far as to joke, for example, that "Mrs. Trask is 'Semper Fidelis,' and 'Semper Fidelis' is Mrs. Trask.... Mud Hill is where it is" (3 January 1868 *Elevator*).

When "Semper Fidelis" sent the African Methodist Episcopal Church's Philadelphia-based *Christian Recorder* a piece that they published in late 1869, the *Recorder* was not as careful about hiding her identity. In a pair of ads for the *Recorder* that ran on 29 January and 5 February 1870, the paper boldly listed "Mrs. Dennis D. Carter (Semper Fidelis)" among its contributors. Whether Carter was upset by this unveiling remains unclear. She sent the *Recorder* only one additional piece—"True Pearls," which was published in the 16 April 1870 issue—and she continued to use her pair of pennames for the *Elevator*.

Still, both she and Bell grew less concerned about her secret; she even began to publish some work under her own name. Bell eventually set aside all pretense of hiding her identity, promising readers in 1874, for example, that the *Elevator* would share a Christmas story "By our versatile contributor, Mrs. D. D. Carter (Semper Fidelis) of Nevada City" (12 December 1874 *Elevator*). A brief biography of Carter's husband in Harry Wells's 1880 Nevada County history similarly noted that Dennis D. Carter's wife "is the 'Semper Fidelis' of the 'San Francisco Elevator'" (214). By her death on 10 August 1881, hundreds of people knew that Jennie Carter, an African American woman living in Nevada City, California, was "Ann J. Trask" and "Semper Fidelis," and that she was, to scores of readers in the African American West and beyond, "always faithful."

So who, then, was Jennie Carter? What did her world—and, more specifically, her American West—look like? How and why did she partner with the *Elevator* to make what must be seen as one of the most significant contributions to African American women's writing during the Reconstruction and to black writing in the West? How might we begin to set her in dialogue with her fellow black writers and with the broader literature(s) of the American West? And why has such an important figure remained forgotten for so long? This volume's recovery of much of Carter's work for the *Elevator* and my initial digging for the remnants of her life story offer some tantalizing hints about such questions.

In one of her *Elevator* pieces, Carter mentions March 30 as her birthday; the 1870 and 1880 Federal Censuses suggest either 1830 or 1831 as her birth year. These records differ on her birthplace: the 1870 Census of Nevada County (which gives the name "M. Jennie Carter") lists Louisiana, and the 1880 Census of Nevada County (which simply names her as "Jennie Carter") lists New York (274, 24C). Her maiden name and parentage remain unknown, though her repeated self-identification in the *Elevator*, censuses, and several other records establish her as African American. She seems to have come to California relatively early (c. 1860) with a first husband, a Reverend Mr. Correll or Corrall, a "Cambellite preacher" (12 August 1881 *Nevada Daily Transcript*). Her extant writing, though, never mentions the marriage—or him—at all.[3]

Most of the rest of what we know of Carter's early life comes from her work in the *Elevator*, some of which was written in the semi-fictional persona of "Mrs. Trask," and such evidence needs to be weighed carefully. Some elements of Mrs. Trask's life were clearly invented: she was, for example, more than two decades older than Jennie Carter. But much of Mrs. Trask's life was, indeed, Jennie Carter's—the house in Nevada County filled with musical instruments (Dennis Carter was a renowned musician), the stories of Mr. Trask's youth that were clearly drawn from Dennis Carter's life, the trips to San Francisco and Sacramento, and perhaps even the knowledge of English miners in Wisconsin in the late 1840s. Bell himself told readers when introducing some of her narratives that "the incidents are strictly true" (13 March 1868 and 12 December 1874 *Elevator*).

Carter's *Elevator* work talks of a childhood in New Orleans (notable for its community of free creoles of color) and New York. She also talks of living on the Illinois/Wisconsin border in the late 1840s and early 1850s, being in New York again in the 1850s, witnessing events in Kentucky's Bath County in 1860, and visiting the East once more in 1861. She gives little—and sometimes contradictory—information about her father and notes that, because her mother died young, she was raised by a grandmother (5 March 1869 and 20 December 1873 *Elevator*). Carter names none of her family. She says nothing about her emigration to California, a fact that is especially curious, given the complexities of both the land and sea routes from the East. She does make a brief reference in an 1873 letter to "rocking my little son in my arms" in 1848, but says nothing else about children (17 May 1873 *Elevator*). However, in almost direct contradiction, her death notice says she had *no* children (12 August 1881 *Nevada Daily Transcript*). Both her *Elevator* and

Christian Recorder pieces note that she taught for some time, some of her later work talks about being active in the Underground Railroad, and all of her writing positions her as a free and deeply abolitionist black woman (10 July 1868, 17 May 1873, and 19 July 1873 *Elevator*; 9 October 1869 *Christian Recorder*).

Hopefully, further research will reveal more about Jennie Carter's origins and early life, although, sadly, most record-keeping of the period (especially governmental record-keeping) was designed around men (mainly, white men). At this point, it is only after the Nevada City marriage of "Dennis Drummond Carter" and "Mary Jane Correll" by African Methodist Episcopal minister W. H. Offer on 29 August 1866 that Jennie Carter's biography comes into focus. Indeed, because Dennis D. Carter already had some prominence in the small city, their marriage was reported in a local paper along with a note—ironic, given her temperance stance—that "with the above notice we received a liberal supply of cake and wine. We wish the happy couple much joy" (31 August 1866 *Nevada Daily* Transcript).[4]

Dennis Carter's reputation in Nevada City and his biography in general are worth some discussion here because they became key factors in Jennie Carter's later life and her writing career. Born 1 January 1814 in Drummondtown, Accomack County, Virginia, to free parents of Native American and African ancestry, he lost his father early in life. Carter's mother, fearing young Dennis would be enslaved if anything happened to her, moved North with him in 1825 and settled in Philadelphia. There, he trained as a musician and gained some local fame; he joined the band of Frank Johnson, the early African American composer and trumpet-player whose marches and dance music were popular with both black and white Philadelphia (13 March 1868 *Elevator*).[5] Johnson's band toured Great Britain in 1837, and when they returned to Philadelphia, they continued to play locally and tour resort communities. By 1847, when Philadelphia's Quaker community took its second census of Philadelphia blacks, Carter was renting a house on Parker Street for $108 per year and claimed both $600 in personal property and a $600 yearly income. Given how comparatively high these figures are, it is no surprise that the census-taker noted that "This man is very industrious ... " Carter may have been married, as both the 1847 Quaker census and 1850 Federal censuses list a woman living with him (her name is given in the 1850 census as "Rebecca Carter"); the 1847 census also lists a young man living with the Carters who was apprenticed to a boot maker (1847 Quaker Census, np; 1850 Census of Philadelphia, 443).

Some records suggest that Dennis Carter came West as early as 1849; if he did, he had returned to Philadelphia by mid-1850. Most records, though, firmly place him in Nevada County, California, by 1852. There, like most of his fellows from the East, he mined—first for gold, and later for a range of other area minerals. He also continued his musicianship through individual performance, teaching, and, like his mentor Johnson, band-leading. By the mid-1860s, he led a band that performed at many of the Nevada City's events, both black and white. He was never rich, but he was economically stable and propertied. By 1880, Wells's Nevada County history noted in its *only* biography of an African American resident that Carter "owns a pleasant home and is leader of the Military Band of Nevada City" (218). He was also active in a variety of black organizations in the state, especially the black masons (twice ascending to the state's highest office), as well as in early fights for equal schools for African American children and black male suffrage.[6] In short, he was arguably among California's black elite. As such, it is likely that he knew Philip Bell before Jennie Carter began publishing work in the *Elevator*. This, paired with the fact that he was clearly supportive of a wife who was a writer and a thinker, provided some of the space for Jennie Carter to become "Semper Fidelis."

That Jennie and Dennis Carter could settle into a life in the middling classes in the black West—with a stable home (on Lost Hill and, later, on Pine Street in Nevada City), a community reputation, and a larger sense of a place in their state and nation—speaks to the massive series of changes California went through in the two decades leading up to their marriage. As historians like Quintard Taylor, Rudolph Lapp, and William Loren Katz have reminded us, though most dominant conceptions of the "American frontier" gender their protagonists male and racialize them as white, the black presence in the American West, and California specifically, was already well established by the seventeenth century.[7] A Spanish census of San Francisco taken in 1790 listed 18 percent of residents as being of African descent.

The Gold Rush changed everything for the fairly small population of California free blacks. In what Frederick Douglass's *North Star* referred to as the "California Gold Mania" and the "California fever," "Mechanics, doctors, lawyers, merchants, sailors, and soldiers have all gone in mass to the gold region" (6 October 1848 and 29 December 1848 *North Star*). Dennis Carter, a subscriber to Douglass's paper, read such accounts (14 December 1849 *North Star*). Another *North Star* correspondent asserted in late 1848 that "the accounts are wonderful. Steady working men average $10 per day, though many times a hundred dollars has been collected in a day by one man" (6 October 1848 *North Star*). Perhaps a thousand Northern free blacks (as well as some Southern slaves brought by their masters) rushed West in hopes of finding one of the much heralded fortunes. While few African Americans in California made such strikes, in some areas and some situations, money temporarily and partly outweighed race. While free blacks lost rights to vote and testify through the Treaty of Guadalupe Hidalgo and the 1850 California State Constitution, California did not—as Oregon later would—bar blacks from entering the state, and it did not pass black laws that were as oppressive as, for example, those in the upper Midwest. Most importantly, when California entered the Union, it did so as a free state. Thus, while California was certainly less than perfect, some individual blacks wrote back that "California is the best country in the world to make money. It is also the best place for black folks on the globe. All a man has to do is work, and he will make money" (qtd. in Katz 106). Even as it included a growing number of cautionary tales, Douglass's *North Star* asserted in mid-1850 that "Gold is said to be found in greater abundance than ever" (10 May 1850 *North Star*). By 1860, 4000 African Americans had moved to California.

Their story—or, more properly, their massive number of stories—has only rarely emerged from footnotes; Rudolph Lapp's *Blacks in Gold Rush California* remains the only detailed study of African Americans in California in this period. That relative absence can be tied to two larger features of our sense of Western history: limited discussion, until recently, of African Americans' roles in the West and a fairly narrow conception of those roles when they are discussed. Foundational Western historian Francis Parkman's notes in his copy of black frontiersman James Beckwourth's autobiography, reported in Katz's landmark *The Black West*, illustrate the basis of the first absence: "Much of this narrative is probably false. . . . Beckwith [sic] is a fellow of bad character—a compound of white and black blood" (29). Thus, Parkman's work, like many of the histories of the West in general and California in specific, ignored or dismissed most traces of a black presence; even in most contemporary textbooks, discussion of nineteenth-century African Americans is often limited to brief biographical asides focusing on the most "romantic" figures. Such moves demonstrate the cramped spaces allocated to blacks in the West after scholars finally admitted their existence in the 1960s: now, in many texts that admit them, blacks in the West are generally cowboys (Nat Love—aka "Deadwood Dick"—and frontiersman Beckwourth) or Buffalo soldiers; more recently, the gendered boundaries of these two roles have stretched to include community activists like Mammy Pleasant and Biddy Mason, although black women in the West are, in some quarters, still more tied to "Stagecoach" Mary Fields and Cathy Williams (who, disguised as a man, served as a Buffalo soldier).[8]

African Americans' roles in the West (and in California specifically) were really, as a handful of recent historians have demonstrated, much more diverse and complex. Almost as soon as black communities were established in major cities like San Francisco, for example, black churches and community activist groups followed. As Lapp and others note, by 1852, California blacks were already fighting for the rights to testify and vote through the Franchise League, and the mid-'50s saw a series of statewide conventions that helped shape a brand of social and political activism that would last for two decades. Such developments attracted attention in the Eastern black press, ranging from A. H. Francis's series of "Sketches from California" that ran in *Frederick Douglass's Paper* in 1851 to regular columns in Douglass's newspaper from Western correspondent "Nubia" throughout 1854 and 1855. Perhaps recognizing that San Francisco had over forty subscribers to his newspaper, such coverage—in direct counterpoint to Douglass's earlier emphasis on the Gold Rush and our own contemporary focus on the frontiersman and the cowboy—emphasized the "Progress of the Colored People," as more than one article was headed. Nubia's 22 September 1854 letter, for example, noted the building of three black churches in San Francisco—one presided over by the Reverend Thomas M. D. Ward, a nephew of abolitionist Samuel Ringgold Ward—as well as the establishment of a "Literary Association" (the San Francisco Athenaeum society), a school, and a public presence especially notable for commemorations of West Indian Emancipation.

By the late 1850s, as a direct outgrowth of the convention movement, black San Francisco was supporting the first African American newspaper in California, *The Mirror of the Times*. Those same early communitarian activists also helped fight the enforcement (and expansion) of the Fugitive Slave Law in the 1850s, culminating in the Archy Case, and continued to work for political, economic, legal, and social change.[9] These developments, paired with a deep desire to keep California unionist in the Civil War and the fact that some key white fighters for the unionist cause (especially Thomas Starr King) were not only abolitionist, but more pro-black than many of their peers, meant that some African Americans in California retained hope that the promise that had brought many black '49-ers West might indeed be fulfilled.

This sense of a flowering and complex black community in California and especially San Francisco, whose later life is carefully chronicled in Douglas Daniels's *Pioneer Urbanites* and Albert Broussard's *Black San Francisco*, may seem quite at odds with most representations of the black West. But black life in Nevada City, the small town northeast of San Francisco that the Carters' chose for their home, is even further from stories of "Deadwood Dick" and "Stagecoach Mary."

In Nevada City, Reconstruction was marked by the final sweeping away of the remnants of hastily built mining quarters and the construction of a brick and mortar town. Very much a Gold Rush county, Nevada County had only a relatively small number of free African Americans, most of whom were initially there, like their white fellows, in hopes of striking it rich and returning East. After the war, mining remained the county's economic centerpiece, but it turned into a more organized and centralized industry, even though a significant service economy continued to develop and some former miners turned to farming.

In some ways, especially after the Civil War, pockets like Nevada County offered some hope as frontiers for black entrepreneurship and civil rights. Some scholars have suggested that the massive influx of Chinese immigrants in the 1850s—whose culture seemed exceedingly foreign to both white and black Americans and who made up close to 9 percent of California's population between 1850 and 1880—lessened racism toward the comparatively small black community, which did not creep far above 1 percent of California's total population until the 1940s. Such was certainly the case in Nevada County, where the black population hovered around 200 (and, in Nevada City proper, below 80), and the Chinese American population, which grew as high as 2000 in 1852, dipped but leveled off at about 1000.[10] The powerful combination of xenophobia and racism directed against early Chinese Americans arguably combined with abolitionist strands of unionist thought and later with national moves to enfranchise black men to create some spaces for community growth and activism among African Americans, especially in northern California. White newspapers, especially Republican newspapers, as historian Ralph Mann notes, were no longer "monopolized by deprecatory tales of low life" in the black community (172). Negative depictions of Chinese Americans were another story, even in the black press. Thus, Nevada County's Grass Valley claimed both one of the earliest black churches and earliest black grammar schools in the state. By the late 1860s, a number of blacks owned property, were literate, and were raising families.

Still, the majority of the county, like the state and the region, remained segregated; in both Grass Valley and Nevada City, for example, there were clearly demarcated black neighborhoods and separate (and largely unequal) schools. Progress in political and social arenas occasionally provoked backlash, and class-based tensions between miners and mine-owners sometimes put both black miners and black service workers in the middle. Finally, because tiny Colfax (a long and bumpy wagon ride away) was the closest the railroad came to Nevada City, African Americans there were physically separated from larger black communities in Sacramento and, especially, San Francisco. This meant that, in addition to limited sharing of resources and pronounced insularity (Carter's writing occasionally focuses on the "he said, she said" of small town life), Nevada County blacks were separated from the key legal battles being waged for black civil rights, including San Francisco-based cases for equal service in public cars and schools.[11] Still, African Americans in Nevada County had participated actively in the state's black conventions since the 1850s, corresponded regularly with San Francisco's black newspapers, and had familial, social, and business connections that stretched beyond the county. Small communities of blacks like the groups in Nevada County thus mark yet another "other" black West: African Americans who attempted to carve out a place among the propertied middling classes in small towns.

Like California, Nevada County, and Nevada City, as well as groups of African Americans in towns ranging from nearby Yuba City to Elko, Nevada, and beyond, the Carters must have seen Reconstruction as a time of personal remaking, too. Jennie Carter left what seems to have been a peripatetic existence for a settled home, and she immersed herself in the domestic duties surrounding small town homemaking. Dennis Carter gradually left the uncertain life of the individual miner, did more work with the Nevada City Band, and expanded his performances and music lessons. Both were well regarded by area whites—Dennis even ran for Town Marshall in 1874—but both saw themselves as deeply tied to the growing black West and so were active in the continuing battles to reform education and to gain and ensure civil rights. Dennis was clearly a leader among area African Americans: his name continued to be writ large on petitions for school reform, he led meetings working for the Fifteenth Amendment, and he was part of most public Emancipation and Fifteenth Amendment celebrations. The Carters' social circle extended well outside of Nevada City and grew from both their community activism and Dennis Carter's earlier life; Carter writes of visiting friends throughout Northern California, including the larger cities of Sacramento and San Francisco, as well as in Carson City, Nevada.

While some of her personal life remains cloudy, Jennie Carter clearly "had won herself many friends" of her own in Nevada City and beyond who remembered her as "a woman of more than ordinary ability" (12 August 1881 *Nevada Daily Transcript*). She was well educated and well read. Editor Bell notes, in his typical half-joking tone, that she was "a comely dame, fair, fat," though no photographs have yet been found (26 June 1868 *Elevator*). A handful of brief references in her *Elevator* work suggest that she was fairly light-skinned; Bell's use of "fair" may or may not echo such. She writes of domestic tasks like canning, preserving, cleaning, cooking, and caring for her husband with a sense of duty, ironic humor, and love. She had a large garden, and even later in life when rheumatism weakened her arms and hands considerably, she worked there daily until her death.[12]

Carter's domestic sense was imbued with a doubled meaning of that term that she shared many nineteenth-century women—that the work of making a home was directly tied to the work of making a community and a nation.[13] As a number of scholars have demonstrated, African American women rewrote this concept of domesticity and the related discourses of respectability and gentility into powerful, if sometimes limiting, venues for the establishment of a black middle class. Such homemaking was exponentially more important in the West, where many settlers considered themselves to be "civilizing" a "new" land; for Carter and many of her fellows, that new West needed to be a land that both welcomed and demonstrated the potential of African Americans. Even as much of the Carters' daily life may seem parochial—indeed, perhaps *because* it was parochial—their homemaking was quietly revolutionizing one corner of the black West. Ironically, this sense of a revised, racialized domestic ideology both explains and complicates what set Jennie Carter apart from many black women in the nation and especially the West: after her work began appearing in the *Elevator* (less than a year after her marriage to Dennis Carter), she quickly grew into a regionally—and, among African Americans, perhaps even nationally—known author.

Still, if Carter's choice to write seems a bit startling to concepts of Reconstruction-era black women, especially those in the West, that she chose the black press for her work is no surprise. The last two decades have established that most black women writing in the East and Midwest often wrote for black magazines and newspapers. Frances Smith Foster, for example, found that the best-known black woman writer of the period, Frances Ellen Watkins Harper, long thought to have written only one novel (the 1892 *Iola Leroy*), actually serialized three more in the *Christian Recorder*: *Minnie's Sacrifice* (1869), *Sowing and Reaping* (1876–1877), and *Trial and Triumph* (1888–1889). Harper and more than thirty other women published poetry and occasional essays in the *Recorder* before 1865; many more wrote for the *Recorder* after the Civil War. The *Recorder* also published what scholars have recently established as one of the earliest novels by a black woman, the 1865 *Curse of Caste*, written by African American teacher Julia C. Collins. A much less known A. M. E. periodical based in Indianapolis, *The Repository of Religion and Literature and of Science and Art*, contains previously undiscovered work by Maria Stewart as well as a host of other short pieces by black women. Years before her novels, Amelia E. Johnson wrote for periodicals like the *Baptist Messenger*, *Our Women and Children*, and *American Baptist* and edited the magazines *Joy* and *Ivy*. Michigan-based black writers like Mary Henrietta Graham and especially M. E. Lambert, as well as the Ohio-based Mary Effie Lee Newsome, made national reputations among African Americans as poets, but both began their careers by writing for black periodicals (including local newspapers) and continued to choose the black press throughout their lives. Indeed, almost all of the black women authors praised in late-nineteenth-century black biographical dictionaries and compendia—ranging from Julia Ringwood Coston (author and editor of *Ringwood's* magazine) to Clarissa Minnie Thompson (whose publications ranged included a serialized novel in the *Boston Advocate* and essays for the Texas *Blade*)—wrote primarily for periodicals. These deep ties between black women writers and the black press continued well into the twentieth century (ranging from Pauline Hopkins's serialized novels to periodical work by Ann Petry published under the name "Arnold Petri"). Some of this comes from the fact that, even in the East, most white publishers were, at best, not interested in "black books"; those few who were, were often only interested in slave narratives (either for political or, after *Uncle Tom's Cabin*, occasionally financial reasons).[14]

But beyond simple existence, black newspapers and magazines carried significant community legitimacy. Many periodicals had ties to organized churches (indeed, many were church organs), which made writing for them a chaste, moral endeavor for those whose womanhood was consistently

attacked in the white public sphere. That the black men writing for these periodicals were often community leaders—most often, ministers—only sealed
this approval. Indeed, the fact that most of these periodicals were produced
by African Americans *for* African Americans also created room for a kind of
nascent black nationalism absent from most white reform papers. Combin-
ing the ideologies of domesticity, evangelicalism, and community elevation
(sometimes bordering on a version of racial separatism that also functions in
black nationalist terms), most of these periodicals allowed black women to
fashion a set of public spaces where, previously, there were few or none.

The appeal of the black press for black writers in the West included all
of these features and others that were somewhat more regionally specific.
Many African Americans in the San Francisco circle—Bell, Peter Anderson,
Mifflin Wistar Gibbs, James Monroe Whitfield, and Thomas Detter to
name a few key figures who Carter knew or knew of—had been involved in
writing (and often editing, printing, and publishing) before coming West;
Whitfield published one of the earliest collections of poetry by a black man,
America and Other Poems (1853). They were all-too-familiar with both the
white-dominated publishing industry in the East and with the difficulty
of making money—indeed, of not *losing* money—from publishing a book.
Most black editors in the West (and both Bell and Anderson were typical)
struggled simply to secure funds to keep their newspapers running—and
newspapers, unlike books, had the potential of ready revenue from adver-
tisers as well as shelf sales. Beyond financial concerns—and though a few
black writers tied to the San Francisco circle (most notably, Gibbs and
Detter) published books later in their lives—black writers in the West simply seem to have favored periodicals, in part because of their potential for
short, up-to-date, and more widely and immediately read pieces that could
be designed specifically for a black audience.[15]

While recent studies like those by Noliwe Rooks and Elizabeth
McHenry offer some groundwork for seeing communities of black writers
that were focused around more open and localized periodical and club-based
venues, there is, as yet, no study of this conception of black authorship, circulation, and reception in the West. Such is desperately needed. Indeed,
given the presence of other Western and Midwestern groups of literary-
minded black intellectuals like the northern California group Carter worked
with—one thinks of journalist George T. Ruby, novelist Frank J. Webb, and
activist Norris Wright Cuney (whose daughter, Maud Cuney Hare, *did* go
on to write books) in Reconstruction and post-Reconstruction Galveston or

of the late-nineteenth century circle involved with the Detroit *Plaindealer* (which did produce at least one pseudonymous volume, the 1894 novel *Appointed: An American Novel*)—the San Francisco circle may represent a key mode of textual production in the early black West.

Still, in many ways, the *Elevator* was also fairly rare among black periodicals. While it maintained cordial relations with organized black churches—both Bishop Thomas M. D. Ward of the African Methodist Episcopal Church and Reverend John J. Moore of the A. M. E. Zion Church, for example, wrote regularly and helped raise funds for the paper—it remained actively nonsectarian. It was also founded in a community—black San Francisco—where citizens were willing to support (albeit unevenly) not one but *two* black newspapers. Editor Bell's initial journalistic work in San Francisco had been with the elder of the two papers, *The Pacific Appeal.* Bell and the more conservative leaders of the *Appeal* quarreled often, forcing Bell's departure. (Bell and *Appeal* editor Anderson's animosity continued well into the 1870s, with regular flare-ups in both papers.)

Beyond these factors, few black periodicals of the time, especially in the West, could boast an editor as experienced and nationally known as Bell.[16] A New York City native, Bell worked for William Lloyd Garrison's *Liberator* before returning to New York to help found the *Weekly Advocate* in 1837. Soon after, that paper was reformatted and renamed *The Colored American*; it quickly became one of the most important early black newspapers. Bell stayed on with the paper, working with editors Samuel Cornish and then James McCune Smith, into the early 1840s and ran a successful "intelligence office" (a sort of employment agency and aid station for free blacks and fugitives) in the city before emigrating to California. Through his journalism and his involvement in the antebellum convention movement in the East, Bell became acquainted with (and respected by) figures ranging from William Wells Brown and Martin Delany to Frederick Douglass and both Thomas and Robert Hamilton. Bell's sense of being part of a national literate *and* literary community comes through even in the earliest issues of the *Elevator*, which actually list him as an agent for the Hamiltons' *Weekly Anglo-African* (now perhaps best known as one of the periodical homes of Martin Delany's serialized novel of slave revolution, *Blake*).

Bell's approach in the *Elevator* consistently balanced national news, regional and local items, commentary, and literature: later issues regularly noted other African American papers like the *Christian Recorder* and the Cincinnati *Colored Citizen*. Continually battling a stutter and never charismatic—William Wells Brown quipped that "Our subject was not intended by Nature for the platform, and has the good sense not to aspire to oratorical fame" (471) and Anderson's attacks in the *Appeal* sometimes mocked Bell's stutter—he was nonetheless adept at politicking in the community and was a strong writer and editor. Bell gained other skilled friends quickly; poet Whitfield and activist Detter, for example, wrote regularly for him, as did a number of political and religious leaders in black communities in San Francisco, Sacramento, and smaller surrounding towns. At its higher points, the *Elevator* managed a circulation of about 800—small in general terms, but impressive given the size of northern California's black community (Daniels 115). With the exception of a brief period during the election of 1872 when the *Elevator* became a Republican party paper, Bell stayed at the paper's helm until the late 1880s. Always in financial trouble—when Bell died on 24 April 1889, he was nearly destitute—he nonetheless created and managed something exceedingly rare among black editors: a regularly published weekly periodical that lasted for over thirty years (as the *Elevator* outlived Bell himself).[17]

Because he was already a mature journalist, it is no surprise that the earliest issues of Bell's *Elevator* read like a manifesto. The paper's title, cunningly punning on one of the latest technologies, spoke of elevating both the African American race and all surrounding it. In placing the motto "Equality before the Law" on his masthead, he told readers—using the editorial and communitarian "we"—"we desire nothing more, we will be satisfied with nothing less." In all of his discussions of the motto, he said he meant "before the Law" as an argument about working *within*—as in "standing before the bar of"—the law. However, savvy readers had to notice the double entendre that suggested equality came first, before *anything*, even the law. Initially, much of Bell's work centered on equality at the ballot box, the school, and the marketplace, especially key locations for blacks in the West; he was less interested in "social equality," which he sometimes dismissed as a "bug-bear" (7 April 1865 *Elevator*). As the paper developed, this focus meant carefully tracking white politicians' activities and engaging an ever-widening variety of the most pressing sociopolitical issues of the day, including the railroad's place in California, the growing Chinese American presence in the West, the uses and abuses of political patronage, and the local, regional, and national effects of Reconstruction.

Bell frequently included his own brief comments, sometimes in formal editorials and essays and more often in brief, unheaded paragraphs.

He could be charming and witty, as well as wickedly sarcastic. (*Pacific Appeal* editor and rival Peter Anderson's name, for example, when it appeared in the *Elevator* at all, always seemed to appear in lowercase, a seeming printer's mistake.) Bell was firmly Republican, seeing that party as the party of Lincoln, emancipation, Radical Reconstruction, and black civil rights; however, he regularly admitted that several Republicans did not live up to his ideals. At times, he could be quite separatist in his rhetoric, and he spoke with the authority and candor of one who had been active in the fights for African American rights since the 1830s. He saw his paper as a key structure for racial elevation, especially in the black West, and, to that end, consistently asserted that simply being a presence was not enough: the *Elevator*, he said, had to be a journal of quality, a journal that not only demonstrated to whites what blacks were capable of, but, first and foremost, a journal that demonstrated to *blacks* what they themselves could and should achieve. He sometimes chastised other black periodicals for errors in typesetting and editing, and he could be merciless in critiquing ideas and policy that he thought damaging to African Americans. He also noted again and again that he would reject work by even his most prominent writers if that work did not meet his standards; indeed, he seems to have rejected some of Carter's work (25 March 1870 *Elevator*). In essence, his sense was that a strong community demanded a strong publication, one that not only allowed the basic literacy of reading local news, but allowed reading in rich and multilayered, politically active ways; in short, he wanted a multiply literate black West.

These values, as well as the *Elevator*'s quality and its place within African American California (and the larger African American West, as the *Elevator* had readers and sometime-correspondents in Oregon, Washington, Idaho, Nevada, and British Columbia), must have been attractive to Carter. Taken in dialogue with her sense of the black press in general, they probably explain much of her reasoning for sending her work to Bell, even though her husband also knew Peter Anderson and was actually one of Nevada City's agents for the *Appeal* throughout the years Jennie Carter was writing for the *Elevator*.[18] (The *Appeal* simply ran nothing like Carter's letters: it occasionally featured narratives and memorial poetry, but its literary and philosophical content was consistently thinner than that of the *Elevator*. Many of Carter's political pieces would also have seemed much too radical to Anderson.)

Carter probably also chose, at least initially, to focus on the local, as she had neither the national name of, say, Frances Harper nor the ties to

Philadelphia's A.M.E. circles of many of the *Recorder's* poets. Only after two years of steady writing for the *Elevator* was her first *Christian Recorder* piece published, and the editors followed it quickly with an endorsement from an A.M.E. Bishop (16 October 1869 *Recorder*).

Carter and Bell disagreed on some issues. Bell dismissed Carter's poetry almost out of hand, suggesting that it was outmoded and depressing (11 October 1867 and 1 November 1867 *Elevator*). Bell also occasionally accused Carter of being too "schoolmarm-ish," as when, in an account of his visit to see the Carters in Nevada City published in the 3 May 1873 *Elevator*, he half-jokingly noted that Carter's decision to stop accompanying him on tours of area mines "pleased me much, as she was continually cautioning me to be careful, as if I were not old enough to take care of myself." Carter, in turn, was critical of Bell's public feuding with Peter Anderson and the *Appeal* and his tolerance for women's suffrage and alcohol (20 September 1867, 8 July 1870, and 3 January 1868 *Elevator*). Finally, Carter was much more liberal-minded toward Chinese Americans than Bell (25 September 1868 and 17 August 1873 *Elevator*).

However, much more often, they were aligned ideologically. In the broadest sense, both would have agreed with Frances Smith Foster's recognition that many periodicals written for blacks by blacks often had to be "undeniably pragmatic" in their sense of building a literate community and had to be tied as much or more "to the desire to create a positive and purposeful self-identified African America as to any defensive gestures responding to racist attacks and libel" ("Interesting Narrative" 717–18). While Carter's letters evince some understanding that whites—she often used the term "Anglo-Saxons"—were watching the *Elevator's* performance, she saw her primary authorial mission as aiding her own race. Thus, Carter, like Bell, treated national, regional, *and* local subjects. She commented with thought and care—and a great deal of good sense—on both the hopes embodied in the Republican party and their consistent failings. Her definition of "local" reached from the interpersonal "politics" of her neighborhood—local Irishmen who called her a "nagur," a neighbor who was full of internalized racism and corresponding self-destructive behavior (28 February 1868 and 13 September 1867 *Elevator*)—to Nevada County elections to California state politics. Late in her career, she even reported extensively on her visits to black communities in Nevada. And, of course, many "domestic" issues she treated using local stories—temperance, women's rights, racism, education— had national implications. Her rich conception of domestic as both "of the home" and "of the nation" and a deep sense of duty to her fellows, a sense that she had to be "always faithful," led her to both public speech and writing, "domestic" duties that went beyond her immediate home to touch other homes, especially developing homes in the black West.

Carter's breadth, skill, and sense of voice in even her earliest pieces remind us of a key fact, one that also makes her emblematic of early writers in the black West and of African American periodicals in general: at present, her recovered oeuvre is, much like her biography, only partial. While we do not yet know whether she submitted—or even published—work before striking up her relationship with the *Elevator*, Carter undoubtedly wrote and published more work than is collected here. I have examined all of the extant issues of the *Elevator* identified by the California Newspaper Project and by a host of reference and archival tools (see Appendix B for a list of issues), but there are several issues of the paper from the years represented here (1867 to 1874) that are simply missing. Most of the issues of the *Elevator* printed between 1875 to 1881 are also missing, and Bell noted as late as his March and April 1877 prospectus for the paper that "the graceful pen of 'Semper Fidelis' will not be idle." The fact that she sent work to the *Christian Recorder* suggests that Carter may also have written for periodicals beyond the *Elevator*, as does her death notice in the Nevada City *Daily Transcript*, which notes that she was "a frequent contributor to some of the leading periodicals that flourished in the days when she had time and disposition to devote herself to literary work." Carter herself mentioned and even shared with readers of the 4 June 1869 and 20 August 1869 *Elevator* excerpts from what seems to be a longer (perhaps book-length) work of fiction on slavery in New Orleans, an "autobiography" of a character named "True Montague." As extant nineteenth-century black periodicals are gathered and made available to researchers, we may find more of Carter's work, although her fondness for pseudonyms may complicate the search.

While a full analysis of Carter's work, including more extensive discussion of the issues above, is beyond the scope of this introduction, using some broad strokes to hint at her literary ancestors, to further explore her place among other black writers, and especially to place her in the developing study of the literature of the American West allows us to begin to see both why her work is so important and why she has remained forgotten for so long.

Given that Carter often used a much-revised version of the jeremiad, Maria Stewart is perhaps an obvious literary forebear, but where Stewart emphasized the wrath of God, Carter often advanced a much more earth-bound vision of faith that was both nondenominational and centered on a Protestant humanism.[19] This also meant that Carter focused much more regularly on her own failings, in part because the persona of "Mrs. Trask" was, given her age, deeply retrospective. Carter's generic range—from childhood moral tale and local anecdote to revisions of the slave narrative—was also wider than Stewart's. Given these differences, Carter perhaps owes as much to black writers for periodicals like the *Repository of Religion and Literature* and the *Christian Recorder*, to figures like Harriet Beecher Stowe (whose work occasionally appeared in the *Recorder*), and, more broadly, to nineteenth-century shifts among Protestant readings of the Bible as she does to figures like Stewart. She was clearly familiar with abolitionist literature generally and the slave narrative specifically, though she recognized that Reconstruction-era literature needed to move beyond such to create new spaces for black voices. She also owes a great debt to a generation of authors of pithy and engaging sketches such as those in the black press by early activists like William Wilson and especially those in the white press by Fanny Fern, whose approach and tone Carter seems to actively respond to and whose work occasionally appeared in the black press, including the *Elevator*, which published her "Why Wear Mourning" in its 8 July 1870 issue. Carter may even have been talking back to two other well-known Western authors whose early careers included deep San Francisco ties and centered on short-form work: Bret Harte and Mark Twain.

The most obvious comparative among Carter's African American contemporaries is probably Frances Ellen Watkins Harper. In part because of Harper's place in the developing canon of American women writers and in part because such sheds light on Carter's gender politics, that comparison is worth pursuing briefly here. Harper's broader sense of Protestant humanism, liberation-centered activism, educational uplift, respectability, and race consciousness as well as her willingness to traverse boundaries of genre and form and her activism with black periodicals, all mesh fairly neatly with Carter's. Their differences on gender, on the other hand, initially seem massive. Harper, of course, was pro-women's suffrage.[20] Carter was adamantly not, so much so that her sometimes-virulent comments against women's suffrage may seem to modern readers far from her progressive ideas on a range of other issues.

Nonetheless, Carter did not see men and women as operating in completely separate spheres; rather, she saw those spheres as deeply intersecting and interdependent: she wrote, for example, that there should be "One purse in the family; not my purse, but ours; not my house, but ours; all joint stock" (5 June 1868 *Elevator*). A wife thus had a right to her husband's respect, company, and, especially, heart; husbands who failed to recognize this right were failing their ordained duties. This sense that practicing any version of "true womanhood" was in part dependent upon men being "true men" aligned neatly with what many women, both white and black, including Harper, advanced during the period. Carter and Harper's disagreement thus was not over women's "place" so much as over suffrage specifically.

Even that disagreement, though, may not be as large as it initially seems. Carter's antisuffrage stance traces at least partially to her sense of the national women's suffrage movement vis-à-vis the struggles for the Fifteenth Amendment. Carter, like many African Americans, was deeply hurt when Susan B. Anthony and Elizabeth Cady Stanton—stung by traditional abolitionists' move to secure the vote for black men before white women—teamed with entrepreneur and opportunist George Francis Train to use racism in their fight for white women's suffrage. The unlikely trio campaigned throughout the Midwest and beyond in the late 1860s and caused not only a rift in the movement for women's rights but significant complications for efforts to get black men the vote.[21] Carter saw her first allegiance as to her race and her first battle as racism—and she was outspoken in both her push for black male suffrage and her celebration when it was achieved. Harper used different tactics, but seems to have shared a somewhat similar base: she joined the American Woman Suffrage Association, composed mainly of old-school abolitionists, rather than Anthony and Stanton's organizations, and, when pressed on the either/or possibility of black male suffrage versus women's suffrage (as pushed to whites by Anthony, Stanton, and Train), she replied that "when it was a question of race," black women would have to "let the lesser question of sex go" (qtd. in Peterson 196). While Harper was, in the end, not willing to let the question go fully—because, at heart, she *did* disagree with Carter on whether women should vote—her assertions that "Being black means that every white, including every white working-class woman, can discriminate against you" certainly resonate with Carter's writing (qtd. in Giddings 68). At a more local level, Carter's models for black women's public activism seem to have simply been thinner than Harper's. Harper came of age among groups that often linked black rights and women's rights. In Carter's California, scholars like Barbara Welke have convincingly suggested, the black community tacitly agreed to split activism by gender, with men fighting most directly for the vote and women fighting more heavily for transit rights (rights much more closely tied to domesticity). Carter bent these boundaries, but did not, ultimately, break them.

Beyond the obvious comparison with the almost-canonical Harper, in reading Carter's work, scholars will want to place her in dialogue with the periodical writers and editors studied in, for example, Rooks's groundbreaking *Ladies' Pages: African American Women's Magazines and the Culture That Made Them*. Like much of those writers' work, Carter's letters "repeatedly gazed back at an enslaved past to battle stereotypes"—"distancing" black women's "bodies from cultural narratives" that limited their public and private place (Rooks 10). Like the club women studied most recently and skillfully in McHenry's *Forgotten Readers: Recovering the Lost History of African American Literary Societies*, Carter advocated for and worked to help create a "race literature" and a set of spaces for black literary production and consumption. Still, Carter did not foresee the rise of periodicals aimed specifically at black *women* (much less those produced *by* black women) nor did she prophecy the social club/literary society becoming a central site of production. Indeed, Carter might well have objected to the emphasis on fashion and materiality in magazines like *Ringwood's* and even to placing emphasis on clubs rather than schools and churches. Some of these differences would have come from her own background, but some can certainly be ascribed to her cultural moment: she was still hopeful that Reconstruction's gains would not be lost. By the 1890s, popular white representations of black womanhood had so regressed, and schools had become so completely separate and unequal, that what critics like Rooks have seen as more limited modes were often the best options for maintaining public spaces for black women.

Rich as these comparisons may prove to be, we need also place Carter's work both geographically and culturally within our sense of the literature of the American West, especially the black West. The first step in this process may simply be recognizing that there *was* a black literary West, one that reached back well into the nineteenth century, and one that most scholars have ignored. Even such a fine recent study of the literature of the West as Noreen Groover Lape's 2000 *West of the Border: The Multicultural Literature of the Western American Frontiers*, which does great service toward widening the canon of Western literature through an exciting sense of the American West as a complex set of "contact zones," limits most of its consideration of African American texts to study of Beckwourth's frontier narrative. Similarly, Greg Lyons's groundbreaking 2003 anthology *Literature of the American*

West: A Cultural Approach, which is consciously designed around a multi-cultural framework, says next to nothing about black writers, especially pre-1960 black writers. Blacks are similarly absent from a host of other texts that consider the literature of the West. Even works consciously designed to push the criticism of that literature beyond a male/Anglo-centered vision of "the virgin land," like Michael Kowalewski's important collection *Reading the West: New Essays on Literature of the American West*, Nathaniel Lewis's fascinating *Unsettling the Literary West: Authenticity and Authorship*, and Robert W. Etulain and N. Jill Howard's landmark *Bibliographical Guide to the Study of Western American Literature*, contain, at best, a radically limited sense of the black West.

Three monographs, one anthology, and one reprint series stand out from such work in their attention to black writers in the West: Michael K. Johnson's 2002 *Black Masculinity and the Frontier Myth in American Literature*, Blake Allmendinger's 2005 *Imagining the African American West*, Dan Moos's 2005 *Outside America: Race, Ethnicity, and the Role of the American West in National Belonging*, Bruce Glasrud and Laurie Champion's 2000 *The African American West: A Century of Short Stories*, and the University of Nebraska Press's "Blacks in the American West" all offer some notable advances in both methodology and coverage. Organized around the nexus of gender and race, of how black men are positioned as men vis-à-vis frontier mythology, Johnson's study offers an important extension of Annette Kolodny's reformulation of the frontier as well as readings of key early twentieth-century texts like Nat Love's 1907 autobiography, Pauline Hopkins's 1902 novel of the (mid)West *Winona*, and the early films of Oscar Micheaux. Allmendinger's book thickens some of the considerations in Johnson's work, moving beyond questions of masculinity, and adds some texts to the mix (most notably, Sutton E. Griggs's works) but also remains thin on earlier work. Moos's study offers a fascinating examination of "marginalized westerners" that includes a strong consideration of black self-publication (including some discussion of Detter), although such is only a small component of the much larger landscape Moos surveys. Glasrud and Champion's anthology of short fiction offers a rich range of twentieth-century texts but is exceedingly thin on the nineteenth-century. Nebraska's series rescues valuable early texts like the autobiographies of Mifflin Gibbs and West Point cadet Henry Ossian Flipper, as well as Detter's 1871 *Nellie Brown*, but contains no work by women. Valuable as they are, with few exceptions, these publications all but ignore black periodicals, place the "beginnings" of a black literary West much later than they should, focus heavily on men, and sometimes echo the limited sense of the black West as a place of cowboys and Buffalo soldiers only.

Concurrently, while literary historians who have focused on rediscovering black texts and authors have expanded our sense of American literature in general massively, the nineteenth-century black West remains a large absence in even the best anthologies and reference works on black literature. Even the most exciting work on the black press—which resulted in the rediscovery of novels by Collins and Harper as well as a much richer sense of black textual production and circulation generally—has often ignored the West. Some of this undoubtedly comes from the narrow sense of the history of the black West noted above. Thus, while Langston Hughes's directive to historian Katz—"Don't leave out the cowboys!" (qtd. in Katz xi)—may have encouraged some select historians and so given us key texts like Beckwourth's and Nat Love's, contemporary African American studies has leaned much more toward Houston Baker's sense in *Long Black Song* that "tales of pioneers enduring the hardships of the West for the promise of immense wealth are not the tales of black America" (2). Thus, as Douglas Daniels noted in 1990, Philip Bell, for example, "virtually disappears from eastern-oriented histories after his move west, and he has not been treated by contemporary historians, despite his journalistic and political accomplishments" (114). There remains no detailed historical treatment of Bell or his landmark work with the *Elevator* more than a decade after Daniels's comment. The collection written by Carter's fellow *Elevator* writer, black activist Thomas Detter, *Nellie Brown or The Jealous Wife, with Other Sketches*, was virtually ignored until its republication in 1996, and it remains not only deeply understudied but still actually absent from many histories of early African American letters and the early literature of the American West.[22]

Beyond reasons tied to her pseudonym, Jennie Carter was ignored because she sat at a confluence of different kinds of neglect—the neglect of her race and gender by historians and literary critics, the neglect of her publishing venues (both the *Elevator* specifically and black periodicals generally), the neglect of shorter forms of literature like letters (in favor of books), the neglect of the literature of the Reconstruction, and the sense that early black literature and the literature of the West cannot be synonymous.

Jennie Carter's life and work call on us to begin to reexamine just what the "literary West" and the "black West" might mean, just as they call on us to radically expand the geographical bounds of what constitutes "early African

American literature." Her letters are essential to a fuller understanding of the black West and to all of the traditions that intersect in that rich and under-studied location. Through them, we not only see politics, race, and gender writ large, but also gain a view of the daily struggles of African Americans, their celebrations tied to memorializing Emancipation and the passage of the Fifteenth Amendment, the questions of morality (especially temper-ance) within and beyond black communities, and their rich remembrances of a complex black past. We also see a fascinating individual black woman coming into her voice, something generally absent from considerations of nineteenth-century Western literature to date.

In part because of the power of her voice, in part because of her posi-tion, and in part because of her choice of subject matter, Carter's work neatly advances some of the most exciting ideas among critics of the literature of the West. Her rich discussions of northern California (and the West more broadly) as a nexus of black, white Anglo, Irish, and Chinese Americans place her squarely in dialogue with the texts Lape and Moos consider. Rang-ing from commentary on color prejudice and elevation to pointed criticism of an attempt in the Nevada State Legislature to pass an antimiscegenation bill, Carter's letters not only offer a viewpoint generally silent in scholars' discussions, but also challenge readers to see California, the West, and, ulti-mately, America, as a space inhabited by blackness, by a blackness centered on self-definition and, as she put it in one of her letters, "civility to all, servil-ity to none" (16 August 1867 *Elevator*).

Her sense of the West as embodying multiple frontiers for Afri-can Americans talks back to works studied and approaches in Lyons, Kowalewski, Johnson, and Allmendinger's works in rich ways, and both her location and her intense pride in that location call on us to rethink Baker's conclusions about African Americans and Western stories. Indeed, what would seem to be her most "apolitical" pieces, those that focus on issues of homes and small towns, are very much about the creation of black homes in the West, about marking a clearly black space within the American frontier. In this, her vocal gender politics, including both her resistance to women's suffrage and her sense that, nonetheless, both men and women had both domestic rights and domestic responsibilities, should also push us to refor-mulate the senses of women in Western literary criticism.

Her relative dismissal and occasional mockery of the conceptions of Western authority and authenticity that are studied in Lewis's fine work even suggest that she offers a key counterpoint to the voices of Twain, Harte, and

Joaquin Miller, a suggestion enriched by the recognition that Harte's *Over-land Monthly* sat next to the *Elevator* on some San Francisco shelves. Carter had a complex sense of just who or what held some authority in her American West. In part because she never questioned her own authenticity, her letters are canny and creative about ways to work with, work around, and directly challenge that authority; she takes such stances with a wit sometimes more biting than that of Fanny Fern or Twain. Further, Carter critically examines authority and authenticity not only among whites in the West, but offers occasionally pointed critique of some of the in-fighting among African Americans in leadership roles.

In sharing what we know of Carter's life and writing, this volume presents Carter's extant *Elevator* work chronologically with annotations. In separate appendices, it shares Carter's *Christian Recorder* work and a list of the issues of the *Elevator* consulted in preparing the collection. My editing of Carter's work consciously attempts to preserve the pieces as they appeared in periodical form: it corrects neither what will seem grammatical errors to modern readers (e.g., the extensive use of the semicolon) nor what Carter's contemporaries might see as errors. Occasional clarification is made through brackets and notes, but I have been conservative in this, too. Nonetheless, maintaining the experience of the newspaper is only partially possible in the mode of a book, so scholars who use this volume should see it as a first step, with one of the next steps being a careful, context-centered reading of the full issues of the *Elevator* in which Carter's pieces appeared.

That need—to reach from books back into the archive—fits neatly with a final introductory narrative and an editorial confession. I had known of Semper Fidelis for some time; I had even read the brief but fascinating mention of her comments on Emancipation celebrations by Mitch Kachun in *Festivals of Freedom: Memory and Meaning in African American Eman-cipation Celebrations, 1808–1915*. (Kachun's work, really the only scholarly discussion of Semper Fidelis to date, assumes that "Semper Fidelis" is simply a woman named Ann Trask, but is otherwise both thoughtful and careful in its rich consideration of how Carter's discussion of Emancipation celebra-tions fit into both national and California black rhetoric.) I did not set out to find her identity and, like many of my colleagues, thought of nineteenth-century black literature and the literary West as near-antonyms. When doing a page-by-page search of the *Elevator* and the *Christian Recorder* dur-ing other projects, I began to notice just how many pieces Semper Fidelis wrote for Bell's newspaper—and how fascinating they were. And then I saw the 1870 ads for the *Recorder* that named "Mrs. Dennis D. Carter" as "Semper Fidelis." As Kachun has said about his rediscovery of Julia Collins's fascinating novel *The Curse of Caste*, Jennie Carter was simply waiting there. Rooks's story of a kind Fisk University librarian who sent a diligent work-study student to check an uncataloged stack of material for Rooks and found previously unknown issues of an early black women's magazine is strikingly similar (2–3), as are the stories of rediscoveries by Frances Smith Foster, Henry Louis Gates, and a score of others. Beyond indirectly addressing the desperate need for more library funding for cataloging and preservation efforts, such stories remind us that black voices may often have circulated in what, for many generations, was dismissed as ephemera.

If we are to have a fuller sense of black women, black literature, and the black West, we need to use the archive more and to build that archive into something much more widely accessible. In short, we should have found Jennie Carter long ago. We should have been reading the *Repository of Religion and Literature* and *Ringwood's* and the *Elevator* and a host of other black periodicals as we were making formative critical statements about early black writing and as we were beginning to think about canons. We should have long ago discovered the black literary West, because we should have known that where there were active black communities, there was most probably also black literature.

In this, then, Carter's pseudonym "Semper Fidelis" is as much a cautionary as a promise; our loss and the gradual, partial regaining of her memory are in some ways emblematic of the fact that research means searching again and again. Only as we continue such recovery work will we be "always faithful" to the memory of Jennie Carter and countless other voices in the black West that we have misheard, heard only quietly, or not heard at all.

My work on this project and my broader sense of what it might mean to be a "teacher-scholar" owes a real debt to Nina Baym, who encouraged me both to dig deeply in the archive and to be sure to come up for air. Pat Latty and Sharon Opheim both aided mightily in the process of transcribing Carter's *Elevator* columns. Ken Jolly, Paul Teed, Melissa Teed, and John Ernest were also especially supportive of this project. The librarians at Saginaw Valley State University's Zahnow Library saved me both time and steps, and the staff and volunteers at the Doris Foley Library for Historical Research in Nevada City, as well as Marilyn Demas and Bill Halliday, generously shared valuable information. At Mississippi, Walter Biggins,

Shane Gong, Anne Stascavage, and especially Seetha Srinivasan have been thorough, supportive, consistently kind, and committed to broadening our sense of African American letters. My family continues to be both my greatest support and my greatest joy. My wife Jodie read the manuscript countless times, commented richly, and helped keep me happy, sane, and focused. Our two daughters probably know more about the nineteenth-century black West than any two toddlers in Michigan; they remind me again and again why Jennie Carter started off writing for children and found herself writing for everyone.

Notes

1. 5 July 1867 *Elevator*. All subsequent references to periodicals are given with date and periodical title in text.

2. The best-known association with this phrase, as the motto of the Marines, did not come until 1883; John Philip Sousa's march was composed in 1889.

3. Correll's identity remains a tantalizing mystery, especially given information I have found on Landis J. Correll (8 October 1822–22 January 1906), a white "reform preacher" who seems to have been in locations similar to Carter's prior to 1865.

4. The Doris Foley Historical Library holds a copy of the marriage license.

5. On Johnson, see Andy Gensler, "Frank Johnson."

6. Delilah L. Beasley, *Negro Trail Blazers*, notes some of these activities, but the pages of the *Elevator* and the *Pacific Appeal* offer the best source on Dennis Carter's community work.

7. On the black West, see especially Quintard Taylor, *In Search of the Racial Frontier*; Taylor and Shirley Ann Wilson Moore, eds., *African American Women Confront the West*; William Loren Katz, *The Black West*; Rudolph M. Lapp, *Afro-Americans in California*; Lapp, *Blacks in Gold Rush California*; Olive Burt, *Negroes in the Early West*; James Abijian, *Blacks and Their Contributions to the American West*; Bruce Glasrud, *African Americans in the West*; Douglas Henry Daniels, *Pioneer Urbanites*; Albert S. Broussard, *Black San Francisco*; Philip Montesano, "San Francisco Black Churches in the Early 1860s"; Moore, "'We Feel the Want of Protection'"; Moore, "African Americans in California: A Brief Historiography." Though sometimes erroneous, Beasley's seminal *Negro Trail Blazers* is also essential. Richard B. Rice, et al., *The Elusive Eden*, and Jo An Levy, *They Saw the Elephant*, are illustrative of otherwise strong general works that are thin on African American history.

8. On these figures, see Katz, *Black West*, as well as Nat Love, *The Life and Adventures of Nat Love*; Glasrud, *African Americans in the West*; John Nankivell, *Buffalo Solider Regiment*; Lynn Hudson, *The Making of "Mammy Pleasant"*; Donna Mungen, *Biddy Mason*; DeEtta Demaratus, *The Force of a Feather*.

9. Paul Finkelman's "The Law of Slavery and Freedom in California, 1848–1860" and Lapp's *Blacks in Gold Rush California* offer useful introductions to the Archy Case.

10. In addition to the 1860 and 1870 censuses, see Mann 53. I do not mean to suggest that racism aimed at Chinese Americans and African Americans did not have similarities. See Tera Hunter, *To 'Joy My Freedom*, for some fascinating comparative work.

11. On these cases, see especially Barbara Y. Welke, "Rights of Passage."

12. The 12 August 1881 Nevada *Daily Transcript* reported that "Wednesday evening about nine o'clock Mrs. Jennie Carter, wife of D. D. Carter of Water street, died suddenly of dropsy of the heart. She had been working in her garden, and about half-past eight suddenly ran screaming into the house and fell into a chair. Her husband immediately came to her side, when she asked him to fan her. These were the last words she uttered. . . ."

13. See, e.g., Carla Peterson's discussion of Frances Harper in "*Doers of the Word.*"

14. See Foster's work generally, especially "A Narrative of the Interesting Origins"; my "African American Women's Poetry in the *Christian Recorder*, 1855–1865" and "Two 'New' Texts from the Pen of Mrs. Maria W. Stewart"; Noliwe Rooks, *Ladies' Pages*; Elizabeth McHenry, *Forgotten Readers*; and Andrews and Kachun's introduction to *The Curse of Caste* for some of the material in this paragraph. Lambert is often mistaken for the (white) Mary Lambert, who is, in turn, often mistaken for black; see Sherman, *Invisible Poets*, 259.

15. See Foster's introduction to Detter's *Nellie Brown* and Tom W. Dillard's introduction to Gibbs's autobiography *Shadow and Light*. On Whitfield, see Sherman and Levine.

16. On Bell, see Montesano, "Philip Bell"; Frank H. Goodyear, " 'Beneath the Shadow of Her Flag' "; J. William Snorgrass, "The Black Press in the San Francisco Bay Area."

17. The *Elevator* was published at least intermittently until 1898. The California Newspaper Project has also located a few issues of the c. 1904 *Pacific Coast Appeal and San Francisco Elevator*, suggesting some realignment in the San Francisco black press.

18. "D. D. Carter, Nevada City" is listed in several issues of the *Appeal* between 1865 and 1876, though Carter and Anderson had a disagreement chronicled in the December 1873 *Appeal*.

19. On Stewart, see Marilyn Richardson, *Maria W. Stewart*; Lora Romero, *Home Fronts*; Joycelyn Moody, *Sentimental Confessions*; Peterson, *Doers of the Word*; my "Two 'New' Texts."

20. On Harper, see Cassandra Jackson, "Frances Ellen Watkins Harper"; Melba Joyce Boyd, *Discarded Legacy*; Frances Smith Foster's work generally; Marcia C. Robinson, "Frances Watkins Harper"; Peterson, "*Doers of the Word*"; McHenry, *Forgotten Readers*.

21. For an introduction to these events, see Ellen DuBois, *Feminism and Suffrage*.

22. Elmer Rusco's "Thomas Detter," provides the best biography to date on Detter, though it is thin on his post-1880 life. James Young's *Helen Duval*, a novel subtitled "A French Romance" that was published in San Francisco in 1891, represents another early title by a black Californian that has been ignored.

Contributions
to the *Elevator*

Elevator 5 July 1867: 2
Letter from Nevada

Mr. Editor:—I have been a reader of your excellent paper for some time, and thank you for your efforts on behalf of our people. Now our children and grandchildren are readers, and to encourage reading, [you should] have in each number a short story for them. If you like the idea, and think my scribbling any account, I will write for you.

—Ann J. Trask

June 8th, 1867.

You were young once like myself and will bear me witness that the sorrows and trials of childhood were as hard to bear as those of riper years. In my fifth year, I resided with my grandmother in the city of New Orleans. A lady friend of grandma's becoming attached to me gave me a little dog named "Nino." We soon became inseparable—Nino being as great a scamp as myself (for I was a restless child, and sixty years have not entirely cured me). From morn till night we played together, and from night till morn we slept together. One morning I awoke as usual and commenced talking to Nino. Poor thing, she only moaned in reply. Poor little Nino and I never roamed grandmother's garden any more. That day she died, and my cup of sorrow was full. In all my sixty years I have had as great afflictions to encounter as falls to the lot of any mortal, yet I never felt keener heart-sorrow than when Nino died. Right here let me plead for the little ones. You to who they are commit[t]ed respect their griefs, though they seem trivial to-day, and do not sneer at the tears shed over their little losses. Their hearts are tried according to their strength.

When I knew Nino was dead and could never play with me again, I wanted her buried. My uncle dug a grave and put her in a box, and left me to bury her. In the beautiful garden, where we had so often played together, there, in the shade of a magnolia, I lay, consumed with grief, trying to pray, as I had seen at the funeral of a little playmate a short time before.

The next door neighbor of grandma's was a Presbyterian minister, and he was a witness to my grief. He called me to him and told me he was sorry Nino had died [and] that God would give me something to love in her place. He talked until I was quiet. I then buried Nino, and he made a head-board for the grave, and wrote upon it, "To the memory of Nino, Jennie's little friendly dog." Oh, how I loved him for his words to me in my grief, and I have loved his memory ever since. I never saw him again. Soon after I went North with my grandmother, and when we returned again to New Orleans he had left. To-day—fifty-five years from that time—how vividly all is brought to my mind. Some little children passed my door. I listened to their childish talk. One little four-year-old, with a tear-stained face, said, "Never mind Etta, if ya did till Tarlo, we see 'im adin en we die and do to Hebin."

—A. J. T.

~

Elevator 16 August 1867: 3
Letter from Nevada County
Mud Hill, August 4th

MISTAKES

Children, you hear a great deal said about color by those around you, see attention given white persons by your friends that is wholly unmerited, while those of darker skin are treated with cool neglect. Such are wrong, and that you may avoid like mistakes I write this for you to read. Let your motto be, civility to all, servility to none. Those reminders of bondage we must get out of the way as soon as possible; and while we would treat all with respect, we should not talk about color, light and dark, black and white.

It is a mistake to think we are elevated by having white associates. Ten to one they are ashamed to be seen in our company, and only endure us for the help we give them in doing their drudgery. A lady told me the other day that she kept the best of company, two families, near neighbors, were her associates, and they were of the first grade in the city. I told her [I] thought she was mistaken, as she was not invited to dine with them when strangers were present, or to call upon their friends unless in the capacity of nurse or servant. Now these people knew her weakness and professed great fondness to get her services.

Now, children, we do not expect to get the older ones right in this matter, but we want you to come up right, for nations and people, like individuals, have to form characters. I wish to impress it upon all that we are passing through a transition state, forming a character that shall tell on millions yet to come, and the world is looking on with over critic[al] eyes to see us assume our places among men. They will not say we have done well if we do well; but it will require our best effort to meet the standard set up. There must be *unity* and *harmony*—petty and sectional differences set aside. Let not money influence us, only as a means of improvement or accomplishment of great ends. Throw away the prejudice of caste and color. Strive to grow [in ways] mental, moral, as well as physical. Let our young men adopt none of the vice of the Anglo-Saxon; our young women have all refinement of those around them, and the dear children every encouragement to study. Oh, that we might awake to the importance of a thorough, universal education. It is already acknowledged we have the capacity; let not the world say we lack the energy. We are on the eve of a glorious morning. May we awake every man adorned with true manliness—every woman with gentleness, and every child with diligence.

Well, Mr. Editor, I see have made a mistake. I commenced writing for the children, and have wound up writing for everybody. May it be excused, with the thousand of others I have made through life.

—A. J. T.

⌒

Elevator 23 August 1867: 3
Letter from Nevada County
Mud Hill, August 8th

RED CLOVER

Children, to-day my heart is torn with sorrow. Its very depths are stirred. I sit and weep over a bunch of red clover, for it has the power to awaken one of the sad incidents of my childhood, and bring it from memory's store-house plain before me. Many years ago God gave me a little sister, and well I loved her, for she was very lovely; ever patient and cheerful, she was a perpetual sunshine in the house. In her tenth year she was afflicted with a spinal disease, and became almost helpless. In front of my father's house was a clover field; she used to beg to be carried there pleasant days. We used to carry her out and seat her amid the clover blossoms, and while the rest played around her she seemed happy. One day a brother and myself were searching for four-leafed clover, when I espied one right in front of her. She saw it at the same time and plucked it. I in anger struck her. In haste I lifted my hand to give the blow. She looked up in my face and said, very calmly: "You will never forget while you live, Jennie, the blow you have given a sick sister." It was the last time we ever played together. Three weeks later she died, and her grave was dug in one corner of the clover-field, and she was laid away from our sight forever. Then if I could have forgotten that I had struck her in anger! Night and day the thought was present with me. All the little acts of kindness I had done were forgotten, while the one unkind act was always before me. Time sped on. I went away from there. In returning years I visited her grave, and the first thought would be the blow I gave her. And to-day, nearly fifty years from that time, I can only weep and remember her words, as plainly as if spoken only yesterday.

Children, do you wish pleasant memories when you grow old? Do nothing in anger; treat your playmates with gentleness; be obliging, sharing with them always. They will soon imitate your example, and you find your-selves growing better day by day. A great man said, thousands of years ago, "He that ruleth his own spirit is greater than he that taketh a city."[1]

—A. J. T.

1. Proverbs 16:32. The full text of this verse, which was often quoted in the nineteenth century, is "He that is slow to anger is better than the mighty; and he that ruleth his spirit than he that taketh a city."

Elevator 30 August 1867: 1
Letter from Nevada County
Mud Hill, August 20th.

Mr. Editor:—I have been repeatedly asked "how I have preserved summer in my heart all through my sixty years." Hoping my experience may benefit others, and especially the children, I note a few facts.

In the first place, I have a childhood (which many children do not have nowadays). I did not assume a young lady's position in society until I was somewhat prepared by years. Yes, I absolutely played with dolls when I was fourteen years of age; and one time a gentleman called to see me and I fled with my family of dolls to the attic and hid myself.

When a child I was very fond of reading, and read many things which now afford me great pleasure, for I am now living my youth over again, by the aid of memory. I still read a great part of my leisure time, when I can keep my spectacles in sight. (By the by, Mr. Editor, have you found your spectacles? I will tell you where I found mine yesterday. After searching the house over, I found them perched above my eyes.[1])

In youth I was passionately fond of music, and to-day I can make music to suit myself. I cannot sing in operatic style, although I get off some very good shakes.

I never drank tea, coffee, or wine—nothing stronger than water. I believe that is the reason why my face is so free from wrinkles. I awake in the morning feeling all right—not like many old ladies, cross until they get their tea; and many men so like bears their children run away from them until they get their bitters. Some women and children cannot get out of bed until they have got a cup of coffee.

I rise early. Summer and winter I am up at five, and endeavor to get to bed early. I try to "live peaceably with all" and preserve a good conscience, then I can sleep as soon as my head rests upon the pillow.[2]

I am not the least dignified. I can play with the children to-day at hide-and-seek, or skip-rope, and enjoy myself with them, and at times I almost forget my years and am only reminded of age by looking at my spectacles, and not being able to see well without them.

I have always tried to be cheerful, able to give and take a joke, and have found a good laugh better than drugs from apothecaries.

I have always had a firm reliance on Providence, and although God has sorely tried me—separating me from many loved ones—I firmly believe it is all for the best, and when time shall end we shall all "walk the golden streets" together in "a city not made with hands, eternal in the Heavens."[3]

I have done a great many things through life I should like to undo, and think if I could live my sixty years over again I could improve. I am endeavoring to grow "wiser and better as life wears away."[4]

In my childhood an old man told me if I would observe three things I would enjoy good health. I will say they proved useful to me, and may to others who read your paper. First, keep the head cool and calm. Second, keep the feet dry and warm. Third, keep the heart free from anger.

Now, Mr. Editor, you have quite enough of this. Old ladies are garrulous, and I am no exception. I hope you will come and see us. Peaches are ripe, and we have an abundance, and would be pleased to extend to you our hospitality.

—A. J. T.

P.S.—I always give visitors tea and coffee, and Mud Hill is a great deal prettier place than its name would signify.

1. Bell often joked with his readers about his need for (and loss of) his spectacles.
2. Romans 12:18. The full verse reads "If it be possible, as much as lieth in you, live peaceably with all men."
3. Carter's readers would likely recognize "walk the golden streets" from Isaac Watts's hymn "Marching to Zion," which has survived in contemporary hymnals with Robert Lowry's 1867 music and added refrain. By the time of Lowry's composition, the song was already popular in African American churches. The second quoted passage is from 2 Corinthians 5:1. The full verse reads "For we know that if our earthly house of this tabernacle were dissolved, we have a building of God, a house not made with hands, eternal in the heavens."
4. A staple of early editions of *Bartlett's Quotations*, this passage is from "An Old Man's Wish" by Walter Pope (1630–1714). The final couplet reads "May I govern my passion with an absolute sway, / And grow wiser and better as my strength wears away."

⌒

Elevator 13 September 1867: 2
Letter from Nevada County
Mud Hill, Sept. 1st.

Mr. Editor:—Can you tell why it is that some people think the world could not move without them—without their aid nothing is accomplished—without their presence everything is a failure? They can tell just what will happen to every one during the next year. (They never prophecy good to any one.) Who are going to die, and who live; who are going to be married, and whether they had better remain single; who possess good characters (there are few with them); where they came from; what their parents did for a living, and how much money they are worth.

I do not know as you have any of that class in San Francisco. You need not pray for their presence, for I believe they are worse than cholera. I have one such neighbor on Mud Hill, Mrs. A. When I first came here she called on me. She was no more than seated, when she informed me that it was a dreadful bad neighborhood, and there were a great many I ought not associate with. Some were too white, some too black; some would lie, some steal, and all were sinners past God's mercy (save herself). When she left I thought to myself, I have fallen in a den of thieves; however, I will try and make the best of it. I will be in no haste to make their acquaintance, keep them at a distance, and they will fear. I persevered in that resolution for that night, and the next morning Mr. Trask came in laughing. I asked, what is the matter? (He does not often laugh, and is consequently very lean.) He said Mr. Rice[1] just asked him my name. Mrs. A. had told him we were not married; I was some old woman Mr. Trask had picked up somewhere, and was not fit to associate with, and she hoped the neighbors would not notice me. She actually went from house to house, telling them not to call, for they might be contaminated. And that her words might have due weight, she looked very solemn, like an owl, and told each one not to say anything about what she had told them.

Oh, dear me; while I was sleeping she was sowing tales; and after prejudicing me against my neighbors she undertook to keep them from my house, but they knew her too well. She failed. And I find men and women here—Christians, and possessed of the qualities of mind and heart that make the true lady and gentleman.

After I heard how she talked, I began to inquire about her antecedents; and I learned she was a great liar, and was turned out of the church long before I came to the place. I tell you, Mr. Editor, her visits to me are like angels' visits—few and far between. For which I am thankful.

—A. J. T.

[Bell's comment:] We have such people in San Francisco. In fact, wretches of that kind can be found everywhere.

1. I have not yet determined which "Mr. Rice" this is.

Elevator 20 September 1867: 3
Mud Hill, Sept. 6th.

Mr. Editor:—Election is over, and "Asterion" is mourning a great defeat.[1]
I acknowledge I am sore. Of course a woman is not supposed to know or
feel much in regard to politics. One thing I do know, Mr. Trask will be home
more than he has been of late, for he has been to hear every speaker—Union,
Copperhead, and Sorehead[2]—and since [the] election he has not spoken
a pleasant word. It is easy for some people to see just what would occur after
a thing is done. I can't see very well before or after. I want to know if you
can give me help in regard to these obscure things. I can't see how politicians
could expect to succeed when divided. I can't see how a man could expect to
be elected when one half of his own party are against him at the beginning of
a campaign, and two thirds at the end of it. I can't see how ministers expect us
to practice what they teach, when they do not themselves. I can't see how they
expect people to be moral, when they puff the most immoral because they
give them money. I can't see how mothers expect their children [to be] gentle
and amiable, when they are always quarreling with them, and how they expect
them not to strike one another, when two thirds of the time they have the rod
over their heads. I can't see how fathers expect their sons to keep from the
saloons, when they spend a portion of each day there, and how they expect
them to grow up steady, sober men when they themselves get drunk. I can't
see why so many colored men must get drunk on the 1st of January in order to
appreciate the day and celebrate it right.[3] I can't see why editors will pick flaws
with one another, when all the world is picking at them, and some of them
will die without being picked at all.[4] I can't see how some people expect to be
believed, when they only speak the truth by accident. I can't see why people
can feed their dogs and are not able to take a newspaper and censure their
neighbors' extravagance in taking a magazine for their wives. I can't see why
they will borrow and destroy their neighbors' papers. I can't see why some
people have parlors and receive their company in the kitchen.

   If you can make me see you will confer a favor.

—Semper Fidelis

1. Carter refers to the election of 1867, in which Union State Ticket candidate George
   Congden Gorham (1832–1909)—who had significant ties to the national Republican
   party—lost to Democrat Henry Haight in the California governor's race. Gorham would
   be a major force in California politics for more than a decade and a player on the national
   scene (as a member of the Republican National Committee, secretary of the Senate from

1868 to 1879, and editor of the *National Republican* from 1880 to 1884). Asterion was one of the names of the Minotaur in classical myth; it is not yet clear whether Carter's reference to this half-man, half-bull was directed at a specific person (perhaps Gorham) or was a more general commentary on the way some California Unionists failed to live up to their platform of, as the *Elevator*'s motto said, "Equality before the law." Carter was especially troubled by the ways in which they waffled—half-men, half-bulls—on matters of race. Gorham (who Carter generally respected) had advocated for improved conditions for Chinese-American workers, but, when Democrats tagged him with favoring Chinese-American suffrage, issued a public denial that some felt went against the party platform. That denial appeared, among other places, in the 23 August 1867 *Elevator*—ironically on the page opposite an editorial endorsing Gorham and his party as the party of Lincoln, Emancipation, and the belief that "the rights of citizenship should be extended to all" (2). For more on Gorham re: the Chinese question, see Gerald Stanley, "Frank Pixley and the Heathen Chinese." Of more general interest on Gorham and California, see Gorham's manuscript "Autobiography and Reminiscence of George C. Gorham."

2. Copperheads were northern Democrats who opposed the Civil War; at times, they were referred to as "Peace Democrats." Many California Copperheads were southern sympathizers and were guided by in part by deep fears of black suffrage. California Republicans who left the Union party when it leaned toward including some Democrats in 1867 were dubbed "Soreheads."

3. January 1 was the day of many nineteenth-century African American Emancipation celebrations—in commemoration of both the date of the end of the slave trade and the date the Emancipation Proclamation went into effect.

4. This seems to be a (surprising) reference to the bickering between Bell and Peter Anderson (c. 1822–1879), San Francisco's other major black editor, whose paper, *The Pacific Appeal*, Bell initially worked for before leaving to found the competing *Elevator*.

⌒

Elevator 4 October 1867: 2
Letter from Nevada County
Mud Hill, Sept. 30th.

Saturday Night.

How welcome, not to the pleasure-seeker, but to the toil-worn ones of earth. I see before me wearied men going home from labor with an expression of countenance pleasing to behold—not the careworn face of other evenings, but a rested, contented look, showing that anticipation is nearly equal to realization, the rest before them on the morrow already half done its work.

The wife busied about the house, laying out clean clothes for the husband and the little ones, thinking all the time "rest tomorrow and husband home all day." The faces of the children brighten. They, too, anticipate, if not rest, wearing the nice clean clothes prepared by mother, and walking beside father to church.

Such are some of the joys that greet the humble ones of earth. The rich cannot appreciate the blessings of Saturday evening, having no labor to weary, no toil to sweeten rest. The poor ones of this world taste joys which cannot be reached by pampered luxury. God bless all who welcome Saturday evening.

—Semper Fidelis

Elevator 11 October 1867: 3

DISAPPOINTMENT
By Semper Fidelis

Where are all the dreams of bliss
   Found but yesterday?
Fled ere the morning light,
   Before the breaking day.

Yesterday I was a child again,
   Chasing butterflies.
This morn an aged woman grown,
   With sad and tearful eyes.

So fail me, one by one,
   The friends I counted here.
"No Summer in my song,"
   All is Winter drear.[1]

—Mud Hill, October 7.

1. In the same issue, editor Bell offered these comments about Carter's poetry: "Our venerable correspondent from Mud Hill writes poetry. We prefer her prose. That is genial, life-like, youthful; it gives note of faculties undecayed, renewed energy and mature development of talent, mingled with the glow and aspirations of her youthful life; it shows 'Summer in the

heart.' Her poetry is sombre, melancholy; it gives evidence of antiquated ideas, and winter in the mind. Do as we do, Mrs. Trask—keep old age away; he comes fast enough without wooing him.—Be young in heart, if not in years."

~

Elevator 1 November 1867: 3

THE LONELY GRAVE
By Semper Fidelis

Why did they lay him to rest
    Where human feet seldom tread?
Wild flowers bloom over his breast,
    Too gaudy, alas, for the dead.

Tall pines sighing over the dust
    Of one once loved and caressed.
The wild beasts are treading above
    The heart a mother has pressed.

Birds singing and flying around
    With notes all attuned for joy.
Little they heed him sleeping here,
    Some mother's own darling boy.

Oh! 'tis a weird lonely spot,
    Away from all human strife;
The sleeper he heedeth not,
    Nor careth for things of life.[1]

        —Mud Hill, October, 1867.

1. In the same issue, editor Bell offered these comments: "We publish this week another plaintive ditty from our friend at Mud Hill. It is in the same sombre melancholy strain as the last, but it is smooth and harmonious. We miss her bright, genial prose sketches. They are life-like and cheering."

~

Elevator 8 November 1867: 2

FASHIONS

Dear Children:—You hear a great many people spending hours of valuable time [in] discussion [of] the fashionable and unfashionable dress of persons, and you hear them regret that certain styles are in vogue, because they are not becoming to them, and many mourn sincerely because they have not the means to purchase some very fashionable garment. Children, I cannot tell you what is most fashionable at the present time, for I do not take a magazine with a fashion plate,[1] but I will tell you what was fashionable sixty years ago, and has remained so until now, and will remain until time shall end. They are becoming to every man, woman, and child, and what is better still, they are within the means of every person—none too poor to possess, and none so rich but they adorn them more than diamonds. They can even be worn at all times, sunshine and storm, in doors and out on the highways. They grace us for the palace, attire us for the hovel. In childhood they have a peculiar fitness; in old age, a beauty that adds grace to the wearer. One thing is singular: if not worn in childhood they are rarely desired in middle life or old age. They have been worn by the good and great ever since I can remember, and when they became old style were simply styled new and looked as well as ever, and to-day they are worn by many, but I am sorry to say not by all—for many children I meet do not posses them, and many grown people, white and colored, if they have them forget to wear them, and so they are useless. Children, can you guess what they are?

Hoping [if] you do not have them you may get them, I will tell you. They are *good manners*.

—Semper Fidelis
Mud Hill, October 1867.

1. By the late 1860s, magazines carrying color pictures (plates) of the latest fashions were exceedingly popular, built in part on the success of *Godey's Lady's Book*. For a discussion of the magazine and one of its major editors, see Patricia Okker, *Our Sister Editors: Sarah J. Hale and the Tradition of Nineteenth-Century American Women Editors.*

Elevator 29 November 1867: 2

PREPARING FOR COMPANY

Mr. Editor:—You may not have sympathy with me in my domestic affairs, because you are one of creation's *lords*, and are not expected to know anything of pickling, preserving, or preparing for visitors. I had just put away the last jar of pickles and preserves when Mr. Trask came in with a letter addressed to me. I opened it and read: "You may expect me as soon as it rains to lay the dust." I was to have company, sure enough. I was pleased with the *idea*. The lady who was coming to see us I had never seen. She was a dear friend of my husband's (I am not the least jealous) and a correspondent of mine, and I felt towards her as if I had known her a life time. Mr. Trask said: "I am glad she is coming, for I like to return hospitality. Many a good meal have I eaten in her house." His words opened my eyes to see clearly that I must prepare something good to eat. I commenced studying what would be nice. I came to the conclusion that mince pies would be rare at this season of the year.

The next day was cloudy, and I told Mr. Trask to bring me home all the things necessary for the pies, and faithfully I worked to make them. And when the next morning we awoke it was raining, I asked Mr. Trask if he did not admire my promptness in preparing, for when she came the pies would be ready for her. During that day a lady called to see me, and I told her I was expecting Mrs. B. She at once informed me that she was an old acquaintance, and a very particular housekeeper, and not a speck of dirt was to be seen in her house. Her words set me to thinking again. My house must be cleaned, altho' it was earlier than I had usually done my cleaning. I went to work in earnest, tore up carpets (couldn't take the time to pull out tacks), cleaned paint, set to right closets, and I finally came to the conclusion that the house would bear the visiting of Mrs. B. When house cleaning was completed and I sat down to do some sewing, I found I was in need of some towels. I went to work to make some out of barley sacks (poverty, like murder, will out). I was making them very carelessly; another lady called. She had heard Mrs. B. was coming. She told me she was an excellent seamstress; her needlework was of the best order; and told me Mrs. B.'s dishtowels were better hemmed than my towels. And she also dressed very neatly. What I heard set me thinking again. I must take shorter stitches on the towels. I actually spent half a day making one towel, when I could as well have made a dozen in the same length of time. Then in order to dress myself I went to work on my wardrobe. I plied my needle day and a great part of every night for one week, when another friend called and told me Mrs. B. was a very small woman. Oh, Mr. Editor, here was a dilemma, sure enough. I am a very large woman, and I could not whittle myself down. I began to review the whole matter, and I came to the conclusion that preparing beforehand for company was useless, for two months have passed and Mrs. B. has not come.—The mince pies spoiled; the house needs another cleaning; the towels are nearly worn out, and my wardrobe—well, I won't say anything about that, for I am going to your city soon to display it. (Don't prepare for me.) I hope I shall not disappoint you as Mrs. E. B. of Marysville[1] did me.

—Yours, Semper Fidelis[2]
Mud Hill, Nevada Co., Nov. 16.

1. I have not yet been able to identify "Mrs. E. B." Marysville had a small but active black community.
2. Bell offered the following comment in the same issue: "We give this week another domestic, home-like sketch by our genial correspondent at Mud Hill. There is more truth than poetry in her description of 'preparing for Company.' While we admit we know nothing of the 'preserving' process, we sympathize with Mr. Trask in the 'pickling' he got in consequence of the disappointment of his better half."

Elevator 20 December 1867: 2
Letter from Nevada County
Mud Hill, Dec. 9th.

Mr. Editor:— "One of the best men I ever knew." How often we hear that said of persons after death has removed them from our sight. Virtues we never thought they possessed, how apparent.—What seemed to us great vices during their life time have dwindled into sins minute, and charity's great mantle is spread over all their wrong doings. Weeping ones recount their acts of love; the public prints their deeds of charity; and the tombstone their age and virtues above their mouldering bones. Their vices, of course, are not graven on stone.

If we judge by the tombstones where dead people lie,
We shall reach the conclusion that no bad people die.[1]

Mr. Editor, I never reached that conclusion, and when I die I hope no one will eulogize me, but simply say Mrs. Trask has gone to sleep. That will be the truth.

These reflections were bought to my mind by looking over some old letters last evening. I opened one and read:—"No doubt you will be pained to learn of the death of your dear friend and patron. She went to live with the Angels on the 17th of last month. She fell asleep like a child—so tranquil the righteous die."

I occupied the position of governess for a time in her house, teaching her nephew. What I knew of her for six months time is graven on my mind as if written with a red hot iron. Surrounded with human beings she called property, she tyrannized over them, exhausted all her own ingenuity devising ways of torture, and I verily thought she then consulted the Prince of Darkness to help her out. You could hear her voice, pitched to the highest key, from morning till night, and such language as she made use of they will not make use of in heaven, and as she knew no other, if she is there she will have to keep still. The groans of the poor beings at the whipping post haunt me yet, though many years have passed away since then. "Sorry to hear about her death." No, I was glad. The sooner all my friends like her die the better. "Went to live with the Angels,"—fallen Angels, if any. "Fell asleep like a child,"—the first innocent sleep she knew since childhood. "So the tranquil die." If she was tranquil, it was after death seized her, and righteous after her power to do wrong ceased. Accompanying the letter was an obituary cut out of the paper. In that I read: "She was a pattern of excellence. Her neighbors mourn; the poor grieve, and her servants refuse to be comforted, for one who was ever indulgent and kind." Every word I knew to be false. They wrote to me for a design for a MONUMENT, and a beautiful INSCRIPTION to have engraved upon it. Here is an exact copy of my letter in reply. "The design of the monument you speak of can be found in one corner of the sugar house, viz: the whipping post, and the SUITABLE inscription: To the memory of L. C. St. C. She thought one thing needful, she has it here."— Whether the monument was formed from that design, I do not know.

—Semper Fidelis

1. I have not yet been able to identify the source of this quote or the figures discussed here.

Elevator 3 January 1868: 3
Letter from Nevada County
Mud Hill, Dec. 22nd.

Mr. Editor:—How vividly you can remember childhood's Christmas morn-ings, can you not? The gifts of long ago treasured in memory. Did you not hang up your stocking to be filled by Santa Claus, go to bed early, lay awake until midnight watching for him, and in the morning look up the chimney for his tracks? Oh, childhood's faith! It colors everything, paints pictures on the mind of youth that all the wear and tear of years cannot efface. There is a picture painted on my mind a great many years ago. It was when I was not quite seven years old. I had been promised by my grandmother a two days' visit to a playmate, with the understanding that it was to commence the day before Christmas. Annette, the little girl I was going to see, sent me word to bring one of grandma's stockings to hang up, for her father had told her that Santa Claus has a bushel basket full of presents ready for us. Annette's father lived in Old Spanish Town, a part of New Orleans occupied mostly by Spanish people. They lived in a large house, and it was more than two miles from my grandmother's. My uncle led me there, and while hold of his hand walking along the pleasant street, filled with men, women, and children, all apparently so happy, that walk to-day seems like a beautiful dream. When at Annette's, nothing could be warmer than my welcome by her parents. A large room was prepared for us, and all her toys were brought there; a table laid with her little set of China, and we ate and drank as though the world had no sorrow for us, or anyone else, in store. But soon we were undeceived. When busy dressing dolls, an aged woman came in the room, weeping as though her heart would break. Nette said to her: "Aunt Prudence, what is the matter?" She soon told us that her boy, her darling, her youngest, was to be sold to go away from her. Bobee, as Nette called him, was a beautiful boy of eleven years. I can see just how he looked, hardly realizing that he and his mother were to be separated forever. Annette and I talked the matter over, and I told her I would pray to God that Bobee need not go, as grandmother told me God would hear me if I asked him. Annette said she would pray to Santa Claus, for she asked him the year before to bring her a wax doll, and he did. We prayed, hung up our stockings (I had taken one of grandma's unbe-known to her), and in the morning they were filled, and with all to please children as we were. Aunt Prudence came in the morning to dress us. Her sad face saddened us, and when we went to bid Bobee good bye I gave him what Santa Claus gave me, stocking and all (which caused grandma considerable useless search, until I told her I had taken it). We cried all Christmas day with that poor broken-hearted mother, and the next day, when my uncle came for me and I walked home, how changed everything seemed. No one looked happy to me. In a short time Aunt Prudence died; mother's[1] parents went to France to live, and where Bobee is now I do not know. From that day the enormity of slavery was ever before me, and all the Christmas gifts I have made none have given me greater satisfaction than the one I gave Bobee.

—Semper Fidelis

1. Carter's 7 January 1868 letter published in the 17 January 1868 *Elevator* notes that this should read "Annette's parents."

Elevator 17 January 1868: 2
Letter from Nevada County
Mud Hill, Jan. 7, 1868.

Mr. Editor:—I wish you a happy new year, together with your contributors and readers. The first passed off pleasantly here. The Lincoln Club, with their beautiful new banner, succeeded in making a favorable impression by their good order.[1] Old Sol deigned to shine long enough for them to march through town with their banner thrown to the breeze. You complain of "confusion during the exercises" on the first in your city. Why is it that people are so active at such times? I think they move about to be seen, and many who have an office for the day are fearful they will not be seen in their official capacity unless they disturb several hundred. The noise and confusion in the theater at Nevada City on the first was like distant thunder. It was impossible a few feet from the stage to hear what was said. I regret that I could not spend the first in your city. The unceasing rain and high water is my apology. I hope you did not *prepare* for me.[2]

I was glad I lived on a hill during the rain, but would have been willing to have lived in a cave while the wind was blowing so hard. Were you ever in the Sierra Nevadas? Now is the time to appreciate their beauty, covered as they are with their mantle of white, the tall pines casting shadows when the sun shines. From some of the peaks can be seen the Sacramento Valley, now presenting a grand appearance of one vast lake.

I am sorry you should be so annoyed by enquiries as to me and my place of residence.[3] In Nevada City, there are Cayote Hill, Lost Hill, Aristocracy Hill, Hangman's Hill, Piety Hill, with Tribulation Trail leading to it, and every one of these are mud hills to-day. Mr. Trask has a mud hill of his own, covered with peach trees, and among them a brown cottage with six rooms, and there Mrs. Trask lives. The first room is furnished with a melodeon and contra baso; the second with a trumbone [sic] and cornet; the third with a violincillo [sic] and a bugle; the fourth with a guitar and two canaries; the fifth with a violin and dog; the sixth with an old fiddle and cat. So you see we live in style, which no doubt all will be pleased to hear, as a person's surroundings determine the amount of weight they are to carry in this world. I almost forgot to say that we live in Nevada county, and there is where Mud Hill is.

There was a mistake in my last communication, I think made by the printer. Instead of reading "mother's parents went to France to live," read Nettie's parents went to France. And for fear some of the children who read the story may have anxiety to know what one of my little girls did, I will tell them. Annette's parents did not own slaves, but hired them of their owners; and the reason they went to France to live, he was afraid if he died his little girl might be sold into slavery.[4]

Now, Mr. Editor, I have a curiosity myself to know who my brothers are, and should like to see Avis, Osceola, Amego, Tyro, Private L'Overture, Waif, and the rest.[5] I will exchange autographs and photographs with them—they direct theirs to Mrs. A. J. Trask, Nevada City. If they do not send theirs, I shall think it is because I am an old woman. Who is Waif?

—Semper Fidelis

[Bell's comment:] Waif is a little fairy, whose visits, like other aerial beings, are "few and far between." "Down in the valley she lives so sly," and that's all we know about her.[6]

---

1. Carter is describing an Emancipation Day celebration. The Lincoln Club was one of Nevada City's black drill/social organizations.
2. See Carter's "Preparing for Company" in the 29 November 1867 *Elevator*.
3. Bell regularly joked with readers about letters he received inquiring about the identities of the various *Elevator* correspondents who used pseudonyms. Nevada City neighborhoods were often identified as hills and were often segregated by race and class. The fictional Mud Hill, here, is an equalizer, as even Aristocracy Hill and Piety Hill (real places) are mud.

4. The practice of hiring slaves was common throughout the South, and such certainly could—especially in New Orleans—include financially-stable African Americans/Creoles hiring slaves. The "he" here—undoubtedly Annette's father—might well have been a French Creole, and he might have feared the fact that orphaned children of color could be bonded to slaveholders by law and that many of New Orleans's seedier slave-traders might not have blinked at simply passing Annette off as a slave.

5. Carter here names several of the other regular "correspondents" for the *Elevator*. Bell was canny about hiding all of their identities.

6. Bell, in characteristic humor about his writers' identities, quotes a variation of a children's song which is still familiar as a jump-rope rhyme.

⌒

Elevator 24 January 1868: 2
Letter from Nevada County
Mud Hill, Jan. 12, 1868.

Mr. Editor:—To-day is cold; the snow is falling; I am alone and have given myself to retrospection, and, oh, what a panorama has been spread before me from childhood until this hour. The joys, hopes, now all appearing as dross. It seems strange indeed that after all I should have profited so little by a life experience. I believe my greatest mistakes have been caused by wrong education, and that it would be defective no doubt caused my mother to utter when dying, "Work unfinished." She was leaving me, an infant, to the care of those who would not control me with judgment, and that they did not[,] the panoramic view spread before me this day fully shows. That they thought they were doing for the best, no one will deny. All have a three-fold nature, mental, moral, physical, and many who have the care of children do not appreciate that fact, and cultivate one to the detriment of the others. I cannot remember when I learned to read, and being fond of reading I perused everything that fell in my way. The strain upon my mental nature was so great that in my eighth year I was an invalid. My mind had out grown my body; then the opposite course was pursued, books were kept away from me entirely, and I for a few years was a perfect romp, until I could not bear the confinement of in-doors, and when a course of study was laid out for me I rebelled, and then they first commenced the education of my moral nature, which had been so long neglected, and the hardest lesson of life to learn—"obedience through duty"—was a stumbling block to me for a long time. My vanity had been cultivated. My grandmother, pleased to show my accomplishments to others, and they unwisely praising me, stimulated greater desire of praise, and to-day, though an old woman, my love of approbation is very great. Oh, if those to whom childhood is committed would truly consider that education commences as soon as reason begins to dawn, and the first lessons are learned from the mother's face, and not from books, and the great lesson of right commences in early childhood, and the first ten years form the character, how earnestly would they guard and labor, how closely watch the disposition, how closely guard the companionship, how careful in the selection of books for them to read. Of food and dress how considerate they would be. The unwise course pursued in regard to my education has caused me a great amount of sorrow through life, and I have penned those thoughts for others' profit,[1] and if there is one thing more than another I desire to see, it is women educated. For the mother alone is the proper teacher for the first ten years of the child, and if she does her work faithfully, she can in dying say—work finished.

—Semper Fidelis

1. Especially given that Carter was aware that Bell was making little "profit" from the *Elevator*, this suggests that she may have been writing for other venues.

Elevator 7 February 1868: 2
Letter from Nevada County
Mud Hill, Jan. 30, 1868.

Mr. Editor—A distinguished man said, "Let me write the songs for a nation. I care not who frames its laws."[1] I say let good mothers educate their sons. I care not what laws a Republic may frame, only such as deal righteously will be obeyed[2] Women alone have learned the art of governing the affections, cultivating the intellect, developing the whole nature of the boy, the germ of the man. Among great men we find very many acknowledging the power they wielded was strengthened by the teachings and examples of their mothers. Napoleon, with a sagacity unsurpassed, said, "the future destiny of the child is the work of the mother,"[3] and when we remember that he had not the highest estimate of women, his words have significant meaning. The mother of Washington said she taught him goodness as a child, and whenever we speak his name let it be coupled with Mary, his mother, and if we wish our children to become great, let us, like her, teach them goodness in childhood. I heard the martyr[e]d Lincoln say his mother lived long enough to teach him the great lesson of love, and how well he learned that lesson is known to four millions of human beings, with their chains severed, bonds broken, and when we talk to our children of the great and good Lincoln, let us teach them the great lesson of love his mother taught him. A great many, too numerous to mention, have borne testimony to mother's teachings and woman's influence on the minds of childhood. Mothers, do you know the first impression the child receives is the most lasting? That little nursery rhyme you repeat to your child will be remembered by them long after your tongue is palsied by death. Whether it be sense or nonsense, truth or error, all you say is treasured, all believed. What an earnestness to catch the expression of your face; they gaze and remember the look long after that face is sunken to decay. When they gather around your knees for the accustomed evening story, then, mothers, talk for eternity. Fill not the childish brain with Blue Beard creations, fanciful objects of terror, ghosts and witches, to frighten them through life and h[e]ighten imagination. The shadow of death is not the darkest folded over the love of human hearts. Death takes from us bright hopes we thought to cling upon. We were wounded sorely; the pain we feel then is nothing to be compared to that we experience when we look and see the germ of evil we planted, maybe thoughtlessly, in the minds of our children has grown to a great tree of vice.

> "Let us guard our words, harsh or kind,
> Uttered, they are not all forgot,
> They bear their influence on the mind.
> Pass on but perish not."[4]

If all mothers would implant this sentiment upon the minds of their children, we should see in human love some type of Divinity; where there is contention we should see unity. A mother's influence at home, in private, and often though she labors in suffering, is great, and the world is better far than if she were lecturing on politics, or taking man's position in society. It is the principles she instills in the minds of her children whether we shall have honest politicians or no—for all women are architects, although her orders of architecture are not Roman, Corinthian, Ionic, Doric, or Composite. Temperance, Truth, Love, Righteousness. Oh, how necessary that woman should be educated. Let our greatest efforts be made to educate our children, instead of accumulating treasures for them to squander, after we have passed away.

—Semper Fidelis

1. This is a variation of a quote attributed to early Irish nationalist Daniel O'Connell (1775–1847), who spoke in the U.S. for the abolitionist cause in the 1840s.
2. Carter's language echoes a more radical reading of the *Elevator*'s motto "Equality before the Law" and suggests that righteousness supersedes any law.
3. A variation of a stanza in "Nothing Is Lost," a poem by British poet John Critchley Prince (1808–1866) included in his 1856 *Autumn Leaves*.
4. This stanza appears in *The Ministry of Home* by Baptist minister Octavius Winslow (1808–1878).

～

Elevator 7 February 1868: 2
Nevada, Jan. 20, 1868.

Rev. T. M. D. Ward—*Dear Sir:*—You did not send your circular to the ladies. I think they would have universally responded to your call for aid to sustain THE ELEVATOR.[1] There cannot be anything in your, or Rev. J. J. Moore's[2], theology to prevent women giving as the "Lord has prospered them"[3]; and none will say they cannot give $1.00. I hope every lady reader of the paper will with me send their dollar; and thus keep our mite cast in with others [to] keep THE ELEVATOR alive. There never was a time in the history of a people when enduring energy and faithfulness was so necessary as now. The Anglo Saxons are looking, and saying we have not perseverance and stability of character to sustain a nationality. Let us show them we can sustain a paper that is an honor to any people.[4]

—Mrs. D. D. Carter

1. As per the introduction to this volume, Thomas Myer[s] Decatur Ward (1823–1894), was an active early supporter of *The Elevator*, Bell, and Carter. His call for monetary aid for the financially struggling newspaper first appeared in the 31 January 1868 *Elevator*. Born in Hanover, Pennsylvania, of Maryland-born parents, he was admitted to preach in 1847, went to California on a missionary appointment, was active in starting a number of churches throughout northern California, and was appointed bishop of the California Conference in 1868. Though he later did extensive work in the South, he always maintained ties to California. He is regularly mentioned in—and sent several letters to—the *Christian Recorder*. See several of the early African Methodist Episcopal Church histories, including James A. Handy, *Scraps of African Methodist Episcopal History*, for more on Ward.

2. John Jamison Moore, who left California in 1868 after fourteen successful years as a minister in the African Methodist Episcopal Zion Church (especially in and around San Francisco), would later, after being named bishop, write a *History of the African Methodist Episcopal Zion Church in America* (1884). Carter's invoking of his name here may be a friendly barb at Ward.

3. This quote is a variation of Genesis 24:56. That Carter uses the story of Rebekah to chide Ward and Moore reminds us of the sometimes radical sense of gender in her seemingly traditional ethos.

4. Although "Mrs. Carter's Plan" garnered only about twenty dollars, it was noted in most issues of the *Elevator* for the next three months. More important that the immediate financial gain, it encouraged women to help support the paper, and so arguably led to the formation of a Sacramento-based women's group devoted to raising money for the paper. The *Elevator* published a reply to Carter's call in its 14 February 1868 issue—from an "unknown correspondent" listed only as "Mary," who wrote: "Your appeal to the public to sustain THE ELEVATOR should never have been made, for the necessity for it should never have occurred, but inasmuch as such is the lamentable fact, you should not have been partial in your applications, for let me assure you the women have always felt an interest in your paper. The ladies do not neglect you as literary contributors, and I know they will not neglect you as financial contributors, when you make known that our mite is needed and acceptable. The communications of our venerable sister, 'Semper Fidelis,' are alone worth the price of a subscription; and also our fairy sister 'Waif' adds to the value of THE ELEVATOR. We all feel a desire to aid the noble enterprise. Now, there are many ways to do this, but a few must set the ball in motion. You know we are few and poor in Sacramento, but my word for it, if the women of San Francisco move in the matter, they will receive a hearty cooperation from the City of the Plains. In the meantime, let every woman forward a dollar, which you receive from yours, truly, Mary."

⌒

Elevator 28 February 1868: 2
Letter from Nevada County
Mud Hill, Feb. 14, 1868.

Mr. Trask tells me to inform you that he does not hold the same sentiments as myself in regard to the use of cold water as a beverage. He thinks water most excellent for mining purposes, but for a drink altogether too cold for him; consequently our opinions clash on that question, and many are the arguments, pro and con, to be heard here.[1] Mr. Trask and I went out for a walk the other day, and as we were going on the other side of Mud Hill our way was directly through town. Shortly after leaving our place we crossed a rivulet. Mr. Trask advised me to stop and drink, as it was my favorite beverage. Nothing lo[a]th, I complied, put my face down to the water, and drank right heartily, and on we went. After entering the town we found our way impeded by two of Erin's sons, with outstretched arms and reeling forms, declaring we should not pass, as no "nagur" or Chinaman should pass them. Mr. Trask said he would push them off the sidewalk but I said, "No, poor fellows, they have probably been drinking too much *cold water.*" Mr. Trask laughed, while I addressed them in this wise: "Gentlemen, Fenians, illustrious sons of the dominant race of Anglo-Saxons, bold advocates of a white man's Government, supporters of Andy Johnson—will you tell me if a herring and a half cost a penny and a half, how much will eleven pence buy?" And while they were figuring out that difficult problem we passed on. The next object we thought was worthy of notice was a hydrant by the door of a saloon. I asked Mr. Trask what use they had for cold water. He told me they used it for washing glasses, and advised me again to drink, which I did, and on we walked until we were stopped by a pitiful sight—a group of boys were pelting with mud a reeling, swearing, blear-eyed woman. I at once asked the boys to desist, and appealed to their benevolence for the poor creature unconscious of her words and ways. Mr. Trask told me to come along, she was unworthy of notice—drunk, beastly drunk. I told him she did not know the effect of cold water. He smiled and we went off again, until we were called into the house of a friend, and cake and wine were handed round. I refused the wine, of course. Mr. Trask drank three times of the champagne, and told them to please give me cold water. I drank again, and home we started, and all went well until we encountered our Fenians, who stopped me, and one said it was easy enough to see that eleven pence would buy five herring and a half, and did not I know it? I told him no, but I would accept his solution, as he belonged to the ruling race, and home we went. I however, stopped to drink again at the rivulet, determined to test the power of water for other purposes than mining, and see if it would affect me as it did those whom we met on our walk. And now, Mr. Editor, I will tell you what I think is truth—that they drank something stronger than water, for I got home without reeling, and felt well the next day, while Mr. Trask had a bad headache, which he said was caused by the champagne. No boys ever pelted me with mud after drinking cold water, and after drinking five or six glasses I am able to tell if a herring and a half cost a penny and a half how much eleven pence would buy.

—Semper Fidelis

1. Nevada City was known as one of the centers for developments in hydraulic mining. See Ralph Mann, *After the Gold Rush: Society in Grass Valley and Nevada City, California 1849–1870*, and Orval Bronson, *Nevada City.*

~

Elevator 6 March 1868: 2
Letter from Nevada County
Mud Hill, Feb. 20, 1868.

Mr. Editor:—The subject of "Woman's Rights" seems to occupy the minds of many men and women of the present day, and we find from the pulpit and rostrum arguments going forth to convince women that they have not their rights. Sixty years ago, Mr. Editor, we did not hear the subject broached. One reason I suppose was that women had other employments; carding, spinning, weaving, knitting, kept all busy, and all women then supposed they were enjoying a full measure of Women's Rights, and did not dream of the injustice done them by prohibiting them from free discussions (and sometimes free fights) in political gatherings and not permitting them elective franchise. Now, whatever wrongs women have suffered, the arena of political life is not woman's proper sphere. She has a higher and more holy mission on this earth. She has an innate purity that shrinks from coarse brutality, obscene jests, horrid oaths, the accompaniments of our election days; and her presence will not restrain men at such times, and women, instead of being the gainer by the contract will be a loser in self respect surely. We want our husbands and brothers to have the right of ballot, and then they can see that we get our rights.

Many seem to think debarring woman from the polls hinders her usefulness. No, there are a hundred ways for her to occupy her time aside from the filthy scum of political life. Women have no equal as teachers, and those who are sighing for something aside from what they are pleased to call "home drudgery," let them prepare themselves for teachers. If today a hundred thousand of our women were prepared for that great work they would all find employment. I have been pained of late by reading some lectures of women—professed reformers—in the city of St. Louis.[1] In order to make women see their wrongs they appeal to their prejudices against colored men, and talk to them of inferiors having rights above them. I think reformers should be careful to govern their prejudices, and if they cannot succeed in all their schemes, not try to pull down the freeman's guarantee erected by a nation's life struggle.

Mr. Editor, do you not think if the subject of woman suffrage had not been discussed in Kansas last year, manhood suffrage would now exist there? All men, and women, too, should awaken to their responsibilities in the world, and try and fill the positions God has given them with faithfulness, and cease sighing for increased honors for they will assuredly bring increased responsibilities.

—Semper Fidelis

1. Both here and especially in her reference to Kansas in the next paragraph, Carter attacks the alliance of entrepreneur George Francis Train (1829–1904) with white women's suffrage activists Susan B. Anthony (1820–1906) and Elizabeth Cady Stanton (1815–1902). As noted in the introduction to this volume, their rhetoric often included racist attacks on African American men—which historians have read alternately as a political move and as an angry response to the fact that Republicans pushed for the vote for black men before—and often instead of—pushing for the vote for white women. Ellen Carol DuBois's *Feminism and Suffrage* provides a useful introduction to this subject.

Elevator 13 March 1868: 2
Letter from Nevada County
Mud Hill, March 8, 1868

Dear Children:—A little more than fifty years ago two cousins were born in Accomac[k] county, Virginia. The mother of one died, and left her little son to the care of his grandmother before he was old enough to feel his loss; while the other lad, at eight years of age, stood by the grave of a father, determined that he would care for his mother, and never see her want if he could help it.

These cousins lived seven miles apart. Every Saturday that distance was traveled over by one or the other of those boys, for dearly they loved each other, and on Sunday, when one would return home, the other would go half the distance with him, and they never parted without tears. In warm weather these journeys were made with bare feet, and I have heard one of these cousins (who is now an old man, 54 years of age) say that he has wept over the foot prints of his little friend, and laid sticks around them to preserve them entire.

This deep affection these children cherished for one another until they were eleven years of age, when a dark day began for one of these boys. Slavery, with its accompanying curses, its inhumanity and its aggrandizement, could not bear to see one with a drop of African blood free, and went to work to make a law, if an orphan child of color was found, he must be bound out to some slave owner until he was twenty-one years of age.[1] As soon as the law passed, men were scouring the country around, looking up those destitute ones, to care for them "as devils may."

These two cousins were together, when one was seized and carried away, without allowing him to go to the house to say adieu to his aunt, his grandmother having died shortly before. Weeping, they were separated, never to meet again, and across Folly Creek, to Tom Joins, a slave owner, Henry was taken.[2]

As soon as the aunt to whom this boy was committed by his dying grandmother heard of his abduction, she started and paddled a canoe across Folly Creek, determined to recover the child. She traveled alone and in the dark, but she failed in her endeavors. The wicked law had made him a slave, and soon after he was taken to Jolly's Neck, and put to work on a plantation there.

The deed left an impression upon the aunt's mind. She knew now how soon her own boy might be taken from her, and she determined to remove him to a free State. To Philadelphia they went, where he nobly kept the vow he made by his father's grave—caring for his mother, and growing up an honor to his people and himself, and a benefit to the world at large—exerting an influence that will never be fully known until the great day when the secrets of all hearts shall be revealed; while poor Henry was filling the position of a slave—deprived of education, toiling without reward, separated from those who loved him, victim of an inhuman law in a free government where millions were not free.

Whether Tom Joins, the slave owner, survived the war, or was swept away with the institution he loved so dearly, I know not; but if Henry Drummond is still alive his cousin would like to hear from him, and if he could see him would weep over him as freely as in childhood he wept over his footprints.

—Semper Fidelis

(The above is not a tale of fiction. We can vouch for the truth of it, although we have never heard it until the present time. We know the survivor of the cousins, or the one who escaped the grip of slavemongers. If Henry

Drummond is still alive, and will write to us, we will inform him of the whereabouts of his cousin.—Ed. Elevator.[3])

1. While Virginia justices of the peace had had the discretion to bind out orphan children (and sometimes poor children in general) since the 1640s, the law Carter refers to was part of early nineteenth-century moves across the upper South to regulate free blacks—indeed, in many cases, to over-regulate them so that they would emigrate. Such measures were eventually codified in the so-called "black codes"; Ira Berlin's *Slaves without Masters: The Free Negro in the Antebellum South* provides an excellent introduction to this subject.
2. This is undoubtedly Thomas R. Joynes (17 October 1779–12 September 1858), a wealthy planter in Accomack County on Virginia's eastern shore, where both Folly's Creek and Jolly's Neck are located. Joynes's slaveholding increased from twenty-seven slaves in 1830 to thirty-one in 1840 to over fifty in 1850. (See the Federal Censuses of 1830 and 1840 and the Slave Schedules for 1850.) By 1850, he was worth over $60,000. His tombstone, in a small cemetery near Bowman's Folly, Accomack County, notes that he was, among other things, "a patriotic and useful citizen" and "a wise and good man in all the relations of life." On the Joynes family, see Levin S. Joynes, *A Sketch of the Life of Thomas Joynes*, and Susie Warren Johnson, "The Joynes Family of Accomack and Northampton Counties, Virginia."
3. Given Henry Drummond's last name (the same as Dennis Drummond Carter's middle name), his birthplace in Accomack County (the same as D. D. Carter's), the dates suggested, and the personal knowledge of the free cousin by both Jennie Carter and Philip Bell, it is clear that the free cousin was, indeed, D. D. Carter. This letter thus tells a story from the childhood of Jennie Carter's husband. The 1850 census of Accomack County lists several free African Americans named Henry Drummond (or close variations); I have not been able to determine if one of them was D. D. Carter's cousin or if the two were ever reunited. Advertisements from African Americans hoping to be reunited with family lost in slavery or in Reconstruction-era exoduses were common in late nineteenth-century black newspapers, including the *Elevator*.

<hr />

Elevator 3 April 1868: 3
Letter from Nevada County
Mud Hill, March 15, 1868.

Mr. Editor:—I have received several letters asking me if I did not believe that wives had rights, and if I was not an advocate of such rights. I will say I do believe they have, and they are God-given. I will endeavor to explain them fully, and hope I shall be comprehended. In the first place, a wife has the right to the love of her husband, to his protection. The beauty of the marriage relation consists altogether in the affection the husband has for the wife and the wife for the husband—one heart between them. "When God brings the faithful man to the faithful woman," and makes them love one another with a righteous, holy, persistent tenderness, which sees in this life only the type of the life to come; when the husband gives the wife this love, and the protection that comes so readily with it, then she has her rights.[1] Not so if he has a divided heart towards her, and others more beautiful claim his affection unlawfully. It is strange how many faults he can see in the one he has promised to cherish and protect. She is homely, cross, extravagant; is not pleasant when he comes in, does not greet him with smiles (when she knows where he comes from), does not prepare his favorite dishes (his excuse for dining out), and even does not sew buttons on his shirts; and some of these husbands are pleased if men speak evil of those they have sworn to cherish; and there are human vampires in the world all the time searching for unloved, unprotected ones, ready to fasten on and drag them down to eternal ruin. But when such forsaken women throw off all that is womanly in their nature, and enter the arena of politics to redress their grievances, they call down the ridicule of many good men. Is it not better to engage in some good work in time of great trial, some work of benevolence that will carry our mind from our own sorrows to compare notes with others, and perhaps our own trouble will sink into insignificance; and we are led to wonder at the heroism of some women, and often great resolves seize us, and the world is better for our having lived. The afflicted hail us as angels; orphans call down blessings on our names; the hungry are fed, the naked clothed.

A right to the society of her husband! This involves more than one [in the marriage], we should suppose, for some women, and men too, are unreasonable. That a husband should give up other society altogether, would be an impossibility. A man's duty calls him from her society into the busy world, and he leaves her presence that he may surround her with all things necessary for her enjoyment. But no man has a right to leave his family night after night and spend time and money in those drinking, gambling hells; and there are other places that men visit, where impurity reigns, where feet tread quick to destruction, and none can say but that this time ought to be spent within the home circle.[2] The good, reasonable wife should not desire her husband to neglect business, religious or moral obligations. I hear a great many women complain that their husbands are members of secret societies. I know nothing of Free Masonry only as I judge by the fruits to be seen daily around me, and I feel assured from what I see that my husband is not disgracing his manhood in those secret meetings.[3] And when again I see the helpless sick cared for, the orphan children educated and protected, I thank God for Masonry, and that I am a Mason's wife. Let us excuse our husbands in all that pertains to their enjoyment rationally. All sacrifices that we make of this nature make us better.—More anon.[4]

—Semper Fidelis

1. The quoted passage and the phrase that follows are taken from Dinah Maria Mulock Craik's 1864 novel *Mistress and Maid*.
2. Mann, *After the Gold Rush*, and Bronson, *Nevada City*, note a significant number of saloons and houses of prostitution in Nevada County.
3. Dennis D. Carter was the Most Worshipful Grand Master of California Prince Hall Lodge in 1868–1869; he had previously served in this capacity in 1863. *Elevator* editor Bell was also active in Free Masonry.
4. See Carter's 21 May 1868 letter published in the 5 June 1868 *Elevator*.

Elevator 10 April 1868: 3
Letter from Nevada County
Mud Hill, March 21, 1868.

Mr. Editor:—"I will forgive, but not forget." So said a lady to me the other day, speaking of one who had injured her and came, in Christian-like manner, to ask her pardon. That she has not forgiven the act was manifest from her still remembering and speaking about it. I do think it was her duty to forget and forgive, after the nobleness exhibited by the offender, for to my mind it bespeaks nobility of character to see a person acknowledge their wrongs. But to see a person, after having done all in their power to injure me, sneak around to every one and say they have nothing against me, and by and by step up and speak, it may be shyly at first, and thus seek to ingratiate themselves—I consider beneath my notice all such. Some persons think they can pursue a vindictive course, slandering and backbiting you, and then come and hold forth their hand, expecting you to grasp it earnestly and with a will. Again, there are those who meet you always with smiles and pleasant words; who never actually say anything against you—only insinuate wrong. Of all the people I dread in this world, it is those who wish others to think evil of me, and have not the courage to say outright what they desire others to believe. Insinuations are hard things to deal with, not allowable in any court of justice. None but the cowardly and contemptible are guilty of insinuating. Still again, there are those who are your friends and have not the courage to defend you when others speak falsely about you; but their silence giving assent to all that is said. All such I pity. A fearful class of your friends are always telling you something against others in strict secrecy. I wonder why they do not keep the matter to themselves—then they will be sure it will not be told. A person to have the wrongs of the whole community poured in their ears under seal of secrecy, and keep the seal inviolate, must have secretiveness enough to make a good thief. Do you not think so?

—Semper Fidelis

Elevator 15 May 1868: 2
Letter from Nevada County
Mud Hill, May 3, 1868.

Mr. Editor:—All women admire the beautiful. Here lies a broad field for woman's talent—painting, sculpting, music, all the fine arts. Here her intuitive faculties can have full play; she can work around her own fireside—and, gentlemen, there are many artists among us who adorn their own homes with what you are pleased to call knickknacks. All those things have given her pleasure in creation, and if encouragement were given, more than one Edmonia Lewis might gratify our vision with beautiful creations of marble.[1] Who knows but there may be among the many young girls of to-day a Madame Sontag or Jenny Lind?[2]—and if not, let all learn to sing for the joy it renders in the household; it requires no more breath than it does to scold, while the effect on our own disposition is far more pleasant. A distinguished man once said: "I can tell the disposition of the children by the tastes of the mother, and whenever I see mothers fond of music, flowers, and pictures, I am sure the children will be lovely in conduct."[3] How proud we all feel of our own Miss Greenfield, and rejoice when the Anglo Saxon race had given to the world no sweeter singer than our own Black Swan.[4]

What adorns our own homes more than pictures? Good pictures have a refining influence on the mind, and who of us would be without the portrait of the great and good Lincoln? Let us encourage our children in the use of the pencil and if the artist lurks there we shall soon perceive it. It is a ladylike employment—far better than small gossip, or contending for our political rights.

The great world of letters is open to women, and those that have leisure know not, until perused, the pleasure derived from good books as companions. There is no scandal, no backbiting, no recrimination, no criticisms of surroundings, and when you close the book, then put your reflections on open paper. How the intellect expands, and what treasures of thought are thus garnered.

Dear women, do not sigh for a large circle of acquaintances; they consume valuable time—and when we remember we must render an account for the use of it, we may well tremble. I read an advertisement one day which was very striking: "Lost—one golden hour, with sixty silver minutes; no reward is offered, as they cannot be found."

—Yours, Semper Fidelis[5]

1. Edmonia Lewis (1843–1911), daughter of a Chippewa woman and her free black husband, became famous for her neoclassic sculpture—especially the powerful *Forever Free*. She and her work toured both Europe and the United States—including a stop in San Francisco that the *Elevator* covered in some depth. For an introduction to Lewis, see Lisa E. Rivo, "Edmonia Lewis."

2. Madame Sontag refers to operatic soprano Henriette Sontag (1805–1854), later Countess Rossi, who gained fame in Europe—first Berlin, then Vienna, Paris, and London—before touring the United States to great acclaim in 1852. Jenny Lind (1820–1887), the "Swedish Nightingale," was probably the most famous singer of her generation; her European fame led to her massive tour of the United States—in partnership with famed showman P. T. Barnum—and made her name a household word throughout the U.S. See W. Porter Ware and Thaddeus C. Lockard, Jr., *P. T. Barnum Presents Jenny Lind*.

3. I have not yet located the source of this quote.

4. Elizabeth Taylor Greenfield (c. 1817–1876), also known as the "Black Swan," was the most famous African American singer of her generation. After touring the U.S. and the Britain in the early 1850s, she again toured the U.S. in both the late 1850s and the early 1860s. She also made significant contributions to black music through her teaching and support of other singers. Because of her Philadelphia roots, it is quite likely that Greenfield knew Carter's husband; Carter would have also heard about her long career through the abolitionist press and postbellum black newspapers like the *Elevator*. See my "Elizabeth Taylor Greenfield."

5. Elsewhere in this issue, Bell noted that "Our genial friend at Mud Hill we thought had withdrawn the light of her mind from our journal, and we were about sending an emis[s]ary to ascertain the locality of Mud Hill. But, as her *nom de plume* indicates, she is ALWAYS FAITHFUL."

Elevator, 5 June 1868: 2
Letter from Nevada County
Mud Hill, May 21, 1868

Mr. Editor:—I have been house-cleaning, and in tearing things to pieces, changing them from one place to another, and setting them to rights again, I lost my second piece on the "Rights of Wives."[1] I have come across it at last, and send it to you, hoping, if any husband had forgotten what was in the former article, he will read it again in connection with this. The wife has the right to the husband's money, to use judiciously. This is a great bone of contention in many families, the husband thinking himself a proper judge of the wife's need, and all that transcends his estimate is, with him, "wil[l]ful waste," and some men exact from the wife an inventory of all articles purchased with the five dollars that they have given her, and talk as if the sum was sufficient to clothe a family of four children. I was in a house not long ago, and the wife asked her husband for two bits. He put his hand in his pocket, took from it, after a great deal of rattling of coin, two bits, then asked, "What do you want with it?" The many little things needed, the wife alone is the proper judge, and it is her right to spend money for the family.

Again, all women are benevolent, and an appeal for charity with them cannot go unheeded. While you are considering whether duty demands the giving, your wife has given the money to the one asking, the very money she begged from you for something she "could not do without." All this, too, you call wil[l]ful waste, is only satisfying to her conscience, and do not be harsh, for while her heart is tender towards others, it will be more true and tender to you. All women should know their husbands' pecuniary affairs. They will then be able to judge more correctly the amount of money they have a right to spend.

It is a very unreasonable woman, indeed, who, after her husband has fully laid his affairs before her, recounted his embarrassments, that will not make some sacrifices for their mutual benefit. One great difficulty is separate interests, that ought not to be with husband and wife. There should be oneness of purpose as well as oneness of heart. One purse in the family; not my purse, but ours; not my house, but ours; all joint stock. The wife's feet are often weary, the hands hardened by toil, her heart loaded with care, and her spirits often droop, yet she toils on, thinking we will, by and by, enjoy all. Seldom does she have a selfish thought. Husbands, can you say the same for yourselves? Does she, in deed and truth, have all her rights?

—Yours, Semper Fidelis

1. See Carter's 15 March 1868 letter in the 3 April 1868 *Elevator*. There is, of course, some irony
   in the fact that a piece nominally about women's domestic "place" was temporarily lost
   in Carter's house-cleaning—and in the fact that Carter's focus, in a piece nominally on
   women's place, is actually on what *husbands* should do.

Elevator 12 June 1868: 2

A Little Child Shall Lead Them
Mud Hill, May 29, 1868.

Mr. Editor:—In the year 1861, the commencement of the great war, in
a State bordering on the Mississippi river, in a city built on the bank of
a river named after the State, there lived two neighbors who for four years
had occupied the same dwelling, and all that time in peace and harmony.
What made this unity rare, there were children in both families. Although
they were, like other children, contentious at times, these little squabbles
were not suffered to break the friendship of the parents. Strangers seeing
them for the first time thought them blood-relations, and when told they
were not, invariably said, "How strange."

After an acquaintance of twelve years, and four years living together in
one house, yet four words separated these friends forever, and made them
deadly foes for a few short months, when one husband and father died by
the hand of the other, and then the slayer went into the army and was killed
in the battle of Pittsburg Landing,[1] when two wives and mothers were left
to care for their seven orphan children. The feeling between the women was
intense in its bitterness, and the poor little children, four of one family and
three in the other, were not allowed to speak to each other.

It was bad enough, but it was hard for strife to cease. Both woman had
friends, and of course both took great pains to impress upon the minds
of their friends the wickedness of the other, and the great wrong done to
them. Thus the whole neighborhood was in a blaze, and whereas before all
had been unity, now were to be seen, passing with averted faces, those who
a short time before were the best of friends; and then the old croakers, who
can be found everywhere, could be heard to say, "Just as I told you—too

thick to stick;" and again, "I knew they would fall out, when they were so thick."

Hearing there was one of the children sick, and knowing the destitute condition of the widowed mother, I went to see them. The other widow was my nearest neighbor, and being in my house daily, had caused the afflicted mother to look upon me with suspicion, and when I entered her door she did not speak to me. I walked to the cot where lay a little boy of three years, suffering with that children's scourge, diptheria. For three days and nights I did not leave that house. I closed the eyes of three children, and the fourth was dying—a beautiful little girl of five years. She kept calling for Amy, Charlie, Baby, and Aunt Lizzie; for in their friendship the children had been taught to say aunt and uncle. I asked the weeping mother if I should go for them. She replied: "Go, but I am afraid she will not come, or let the children come."

The hardest pleading I have done in all my life was with my neighbor. As fast as she made excuses I told her I was sent by an angel and she must go with me, and at last I prevailed. When we entered the door, the little dying girl raised her head from the pillow, reached out both arms—and oh! the kisses she gave them with her cold lips; then calling her mother, said: "Kiss aunt Lizzie, ma, for me."

I saw that kiss, and after that I could not see, for tears blinded my eyes. The dear little child lay back on her pillow, saying: "Ain't this nice! Ain't this nice," and laying her hands across her breast, she died.

Mr. Editor, this is no tale of fiction:—every word is truth.[2] Both mothers have lately come to California with the three children, the childless widow caring for those children as if they were her own; and the love these women bear for one another is time enduring.

—Yours, Semper Fidelis

1. Better known as the Battle of Shiloh, the Battle of Pittsburg Landing—waged on 6 and 7 April 1862, months before the enlistment of black troops in the Union army was officially allowed—was one of the bloodiest battles of the Civil War.
2. Carter's language here is a reminder that the nineteenth-century literary investment in the death scene was often rooted in reality.

Elevator 3 July 1868: 2

LETTER TO MR. TRASK
San Francisco, June 29, 1868

Dear Darby:—You wished me to give you my impressions of this great city—what I thought of the influence of our people here, of the talent among them, and of our Editor. The first thing I noticed as peculiar to San Francisco was, that it is not morning when the sun rises; it is not really morning until after nine o'clock. I have been told there are many people living here who never saw the sun rise, and while we are expending sympathy on the poor English miners, who are compelled to toil year after year under ground, shut out from sight of the glorious orb of day, let us drop a tear for the people who here are bound by Fashion's stern decree not during a lifetime to see the sun rise.

Of the influence exerted by the colored people, I can say but little. Divisions are always painful, and when our people in this city are but as a mite in a mountain, to see them cut up into factions and cliques is cause for sadness. I despaired years ago of union being brought about by the different churches. My great hope was in Masonry; but since I came here I have ceased to cherish that idea, and now my only hope is in the growing intelligence of our youth.[1]

There is native talent here, but I see the same mistake as in other places—stopping at "well done," not thinking there is a "better best." It will not do for us to abide by the decision of the people around us for many of them have talked of inferiority, and are ready to say we have done beautifully when we have only half done, for fear of superiority.

Mr. Bell, our Editor, is an old gentleman of good mind and cultivation—of rough exterior, impulsive, slightly given to boasting of his vigor at sixty, fond of wit and wine, not fond of women, unforgiving to his enemies, loving his friends, somewhat imprudent as an editor—praising and overrating the talents of his contributors, making them satisfied with their compositions instead of provoking them to greater application.[2] I wish he would make "Semper Fidelis" write better, "Waif" oftener, and "Osceola" only for THE ELEVATOR.[3]

In my next I will give you an account of my reflections further.

—Yours, Semper Fidelis
(Otherwise Joan Trask)

1. As she continued writing, Carter became more and more critical of rifts in San Francisco's black community, especially the significant antagonism between Bell and rival editor Peter Anderson, some of which was played out in black masonry circles.

2. This passage can be seen as Carter's playful response to Bell's description (in the 26 June 1868 *Elevator*) of her at their first meeting as "fat, fair, and not forty." Useful comparison can be made to Martin Delany's 1852 description of Bell in *The Condition, Elevation, Emigration, and Destiny of the Colored People of the U.S.*: "Mr. Bell is an excellent business man, talented, prompt, shrewd, and full of tact. And what seems to be a trait of character only to be associated with talent, Mr. Bell is highly sensitive and very eccentric" (103).

3. "Waif" and "Osceola" were two other writers for the *Elevator*; I have not yet identified them.

~

Elevator 10 July 1868: 1

Letter To Mr. Trask
San Francisco, July 4, 1868

Dear Darby: The patriotism of this city is great, if "star spangled banners" are any evidence of love of country. To-day, when I saw in the procession a milk wagon covered with the dear old flag, I thought it might possibly be used to cover up dirt—and after reflecting upon the subject, I have come to the conclusion that there is very little patriotism in California, and that all this display is a farce. I have not had one good feeling this day, for I have looked upon wrong—bitter wrong. In this city is a military company—the Brannan Guards—soldierly men, as well disciplined as any in the city; yet they were not in the procession, and I understand they asked for a position—wrote to the Marshal, and he never replied to their note.[1] O! for a Lincoln at the head of this nation, and a Starr King in this city.[2] If I were a man, I would not cease crying until they said either yes or no. If the flag is thick enough to cover the ignorance of Irishmen, it certainly ought to cover our dark skins. Do you think we are in earnest as regards our rights? An Anglo Saxon editor of this city, told me a year ago, in our home at Mud Hill, that he was fearful our people had not the energy to elevate themselves. Is it true? Are we quietly submitting to insult and neglect, deprived of rights of place and position, without raising a note of indignation?

I visited San Jose, and attended the concert given by Mr. Cassey's pupils. I also visited the Institute, but the school was not in session, so I heard no recitations.[3] I think they have demonstrated the musical ability of their pupils. I do not believe there is in San Jose the same number of white children, with the same advantages, who could have done as well. Mr. Cassey has spent time and money to establish a school, but I hear it is poorly sustained. The necessity of concerts and exhibitions ought not to exist; in my experience as a teacher, I have found them deleterious; children's minds are diverted from their studies before and after.[4]—A yearly examination I would not censure, but approve; and while music has a softening and refining influence on the mind, I feel anxious for our children to excel in mathematics, for there lays the foundation of every science. Again, I would say to the teacher, watch the child's inclination to study, and you will discover whether the mechanic, musician or orator is in embryo before you.

Thousands of dollars are spent yearly to make children musicians who have no love for music, and who never will excel as musicians, while that money and time employed judiciously would make engineers, mechanics, artists or statesmen.

I feel that our people are asleep on the subject of education in this city, or they would not submit to an order from chivalry's headquarters, which reads; "The public schools of this city will open on the 6th of July, except the colored school." How long, O lord! how long, must we tamely submit to all this injustice? Must our children grow up in ignorance, to make true their estimate of inferiority? If I were a man, I would battle until death; but as I am merely Mrs. Trask, I will have to keep in my place. They cannot prevent me from talking and writing, and my tongue and pen shall be busy.

—Yours, Semper Fidelis.
(Otherwise Joan Trask.)

1. The Brannan Guards were perhaps the most famous of the black drill organizations in San Francisco. They were regular participants in Emancipation Day celebrations, and their activities were often mentioned in the *Elevator*.
2. Thomas Starr King (1824–1864) was a white Unitarian minister who came to the San Francisco area early in 1860 and passionately spread not only a Unitarian Universalist message but also a strong unionist ethos. General Winfield Scott reportedly claimed that Starr King "saved California for the Union" at the outbreak of the Civil War, and, in part because of this work, Starr King gained great popularity with California's black community. See Rudolph M. Lapp and Robert J. Chandler, "The Antiracism of Thomas Starr King."
3. Carter here refers to Peter William Cassey (1831–?), the son of Philadelphia black abolitionist Joseph Cassey. Peter Cassey initially settled in San Francisco and worked as a barber, but moved to San Jose, where he became an Episcopalian minister and educator. The "Institute" Carter notes is the Phoenixonian Institute, California's first secondary school for African Americans, which Cassey founded in San Jose. On Cassey, see Lionel Utley Ridout's "The Church, the Chinese, and the Negroes in California."

4. Though it had both church ties and vocal support from black activists (including, sometimes, the *Elevator*), the Phoenixonian Institute struggled financially. Because of this—and the need for good publicity—the Institute staged such exhibitions with some regularity.

~

Elevator 31 July 1868: 1

LETTER TO MR. TRASK.
San Francisco, July 24 [1868]

Dear Darby: The agitation on the school question in this city is truly hopeful. The spirit manifested at the public meetings I have attended bespeaks attention from the public mind, and while the Board of Public Instruction may feel an indifference towards us, public opinion will force them to do us justice.[1] In view of that fact would it not be well to first divest ourselves of prejudice in regard to color. My ears are continually pained by expressions like these: "Great big black nigger," "You yeller trash," "They think they are white." Now, all this is wrong, unbecoming, disgraceful. The feelings we display our children will manifest towards each other. We should remember the same God created us; we are all alike; the only difference is in the improvement we make of our time; all the hours spent discussing shades are lost; we are only gratifying our selfish propensities, while the same time appropriated to reading would help to enlarge our ideas of each other and mankind in general.—What we can accomplish for ourselves alone in this world is no matter, let us throw aside self entirely, labor for great principles which will bless all—for you know, D., there are many of whom more might be made; many a one with high hopes and aspirations suddenly crushed by a selfish act, and gone down to the grave deg[r]aded and their memory only a shame.

The people of this city are far behind their opportunities. Soon they will have a fearful awakening. The selfish spirit[s] manifested by the different churches, Masonic organizations and neighborhood cliques are greater than I dreamed of, and while there are many noble souls who are ever alive to the public good, whose whole aim is unselfish, the selfishness of others hinders their work.

I am happy in having made the acquaintance of "Waif," "Osceola," and "Avis"—all tried workers for humanity, and many dear friends, who have made my stay in this city so pleasant that Mud Hill seems dull indeed to

—Yours, Semper Fidelis
(Otherwise Joan Trask.)

1. San Francisco was a center of California blacks' attempts to gain fair school funding under state law. Dennis Carter was a long-time activist on the issue, and he and Bell worked together on petition drives and other activities. See Daniels, *Pioneer Urbanites*, and Beasley, *Negro Trail Blazers*.

~

Elevator 7 August 1868: 1

LETTER TO MR. TRASK
San Francisco, August 4, 1868

Dear Darby:—I must still scold, and I am such a persistent fault-finder, I am fearful I may have to flee to the mountains for security. Yesterday, I attended the celebration at Hayes Park, and while I saw much to enjoy, my soul was tried beyond all reason.[1] In the first place, the exercises of the day were appointed to commence at 11 o'clock; hour after hour passed away before the people were called to listen to the opening remarks of the President of the day, Wm. Hall. That they were good, I do not doubt, as all that gentlemen says in public is good.[2] While I was seated near the speaker, and intensely straining my ears to listen, I could not hear one-half [of what] he said. The confusion was dreadful; people walking, and children running across the floor, and even some who profess to be ladies, indulging in loud conversation, interspersed with laughter.

Several of the speakers I did not understand one word they said. The oration by Mr. Collouch was pronounced excellent by those who heard it, also the addresses of Messrs. R. Hall, S. Howard and Charlton.[3] The poem I did not hear, for during the reading of it, all the lads and misses in the house went into the garden, some of them accompanied by their parents. When I tell you by indignation was aroused, I am only half saying what I felt.

If parents cannot instruct their children to obey the laws of civility and politeness, and if they themselves cannot exercise respect for persons and place, I see no chance of our ever rising up to take a position with those around us. If people do not desire to listen, let them remain away, not destroy the pleasure of others, and if an appointment it made, let it be observed. If the exercises of the day commence at the appointed time, it will insure prompt attendance in future. The observance of a day, so hallowed to many hearts, commemorative to freedom's first jubilee, should be kept in a sane, rational manner, without noise and confusion, drunkenness or its attendant indecencies and vulgarity. God help us all to be true men and women, that the world may be better for our having lived.— Yours,

—Semper Fidelis

1. August 1 was often celebrated by African Americans in commemoration of the emancipation of slaves in the British West Indies. San Francisco regularly held such gatherings at Hayes Park, including an especially large gathering on 1 September 1862. See Kachun, *Festivals of Freedom*, 123–124 on this celebration.
2. Born free in Washington, D.C., c. 1823, William H. Hall moved to New York as a child, attended Oberlin for two years, and went to California in 1849. His financial success brought him back to New York to marry in 1851, but he returned with his wife to California in 1854, where he worked as a barber in San Francisco. A longtime activist, he, among other roles, chaired the 1857 California State Convention of Colored Citizens and was the first president of the San Francisco Literary Institute. Basic information on his biography can be found in Delilah L. Beasley's *Negro Trail Blazers of California*.
3. I have not yet identified Collouch. Charlton may be C. C. C. Charlton (c. 1851–?), a barber born in the West Indies; see 1880 Census of Nevada County, California, 1A and 44B. R. Hall was R. A. Hall, who was active in a range of causes alongside Philip Bell but left little biographical record. S. Howard—Shadrack Howard (c. 1820–?), owner of a hydraulic hose factory in San Francisco and one of the city's leading black businessmen—gave the closing address. James Whitfield recited an original poem at the festivities.

⌒

Elevator 21 August 1868: 2

THE MISSION OF MASONRY
A POEM
Written and Delivered by Mrs. D.D. Carter of Nevada City, at the Masonic Festival
August 11, 1868

A dreamer gave a golden thought:
On seraph's wings it flew;

The thought was all divine—
 Was old and yet was new.

It traversed space and time,
 Through ages dark and sere—
Bore fruit in every clime,
 And dear as life was dear.

It entered into halls of wealth,
 'Mid treasures manifold;
It entered not by stealth,
 It entered not for gold.

It entered in where bloody strife
 Had severed brothers dear—
Taught that, instead of spite,
 A brother's faults to bear.

It entered where the man of want
 Lay stretched on couch of pain;
With ready hand it raised him up
 To manhood's strength again.

It entered where the widow dwelt,
 With all her children poor,
And saved her from a life of toil,
 To beg from door to door.

It entered in the orphan's home,
 Bereft of earthly care;
It raised up a Father's hand,
 Their sorrows all to share.

It entered where the man of sin
 By conscience goaded fled,
And taught him to embrace a life
 Of holiness instead.

In Science's name it temples reared,
 Man's ignorance to dispel—
By the plummet and the square,
 Securely built and well.

The castle on the lofty hill,
    The cottage on the lea,—
Welcomed with a ready hand
    The truths of Masonry.

A thought so fraught with good
    To all beneath the rod,
Must have its birth in Heaven—
    Must emanate from God.

⌒

Elevator 11 September 1868: 2
Letter from Nevada County
Mud Hill, September 2, 1868

Mr. Editor:—Politicians may rant (at least some of them—the sweet sons of modern Democracy), and talk loud and strong of the good old days of slavery, when the "nigger" was in his right place, cared for by kind masters (and in those days all were kind), and regret, as I heard one of them the other day, the suffering of the colored people South since the war. I was in no mood to answer him, knowing that he, in common with other Democrats, had no use for the negro aside from servitude, and all his sympathy was the merest sham.[1] In the company prese[n]t was a colored woman fifty years old, and she asked for the privilege of telling a story, which was readily granted.

She said she was born in the State of Alabama,—was born free, her mother being a free woman and her father a slave. The law of that State required all free born children of color to have guardians, parents counting as nothing under that most beautiful system.

When she was thirteen years of age, a noted divine, a slave owner and a near neighbor of her guardians, tendered her an invitation to accompany him to New Orleans. He had gained the consent of her guardian before asking her, and in glowing colors the trip was painted, and the fine things to be bought for her when once in the city. Girl-like she believed what was told her, and with trusting faith packed her box of clothes, and bade her weeping mother good-bye with tearless eyes for the journey of three months, as waiting-maid for the Rev. Mrs. B_____m.[2] I often wonder why there is no pitying angel standing by to stop one when men and devils conspire against them.

Six long months passed, and yet the fond mother heard not from her child.—When nearly a year had passed, home came the Rev. B_____m, accompanied by his wife, but not the servant. He sent for the mother, and with a full heart told her of the happy death of her daughter—gave her her dying message, appointed a time to preach to the servants, and then with language most pathetic he told the story of the girl's conversion, sickness and triumphant death, delivering her last request to all to meet her in heaven,—and one united "I will" went up with wailing to be recorded above.

Three years went by, the mother's grief growing less as time rolled on. During the time of Mr. B.'s absence the guardian visited New Orleans, and on his return the mother asked if he had seen her child, and he replied, "No, I did not look for her." But now he had a daughter grown, and some insult was offered her by this Rev. B_____m. Forthwith he started to New Orleans, and soon as possible returned with a pitiable object of humanity.

It was twilight when he arrived in F_____ville. He sent a servant for the girl's mother, one for the minister, and one for those she had associated with. The beatings about the head which the girl had received, and the hardships she had endured, had destroyed her memory of former days and faces. She did not know her guardian who had brought her home—did not know her mother; but the minister who had sold her and reported her death knew her, and the sight appalled him; he fainted, and then his wife informed them how she had begged him not to sell the girl, thus convicting her husband.

The scene baffled description, and it was a long time before that girl's memory was restored to her, and what she suffered made a life impression upon her mind.—She, as a woman of fifty years, with this experience ever present, wished to impress it upon the minds of all. The sympathy the Democrats feel for the colored people at the South was the same her old guardian felt for her. He knew she was sold a slave, yet did not make any attempt for her freedom until he had hatred to gratify; and it was the hatred to the Radicals that made the Democrats so tender-hearted, so ready to weep over the poor negro.

—Semper Fidelis

1. Carter was merciless in attacking the lies of California Democrats, whose pro-Southern, pro-reconciliation, and deeply racist policies she saw as a great threat to black civil rights.

2. In her 18 October 1868 letter, published in the 23 October 1868 *Elevator*, Carter identifies
   the surname as Bingham and the "F____ville" mentioned later in the place as Fayetteville,
   Mississippi. I have not yet been able to identify those involved in this narrative.

⌒

Elevator 25 September 1868: 2
Letter from Nevada County
Mud Hill, Sept. 12, 1868

Mr. Editor:—There is in the present political campaign less bitterness than
heretofore at the North, while at the South it is increased ten-fold. A Democrat said the other day, that the feeling exhibited South was "caused by
negroes seeking equality, and the people would not endure it and the despotism it brought them." They can't stand despotism. I think they ought to,
for they have dealt largely in that material. Until the rebellion, who dared
to express an opinion adverse to human bondage south of Mason and Dix-
on's line? Who dared read the first clause of the Constitution—"All men are
born free and equal"—and give it a literal interpretation? And who dared
preach the whole gospel—that master and servant were equal? Who dared
to be seen reading the New York *Tribune*.[1] All must put a lock on their lips,
or suffer imprisonment and death. I know what I write, having spent a great
portion of my life there; and often have I been told if I were a man I would
be hung: and for what? Why, for saying slavery was wrong.

I recollect one time, in B____ county, Kentucky,[2] I sat up all night
with a poor slave mother, who lay in spasms, caused by the selling to a negro
trader of her little boy, not three years of age. When in the morning her
master came to her cabin to see how she was, I began to plead with him in
humanity's name; and when that would not move him, I told him God was
just, and would not suffer such things forever. He told me I had said enough
to hang me.

They had better not talk of despotism and military rule now. I am sure
they have more liberty than they ever allowed others. They can all speak their
minds fully—even curse the Government that ought to have hung them;
and now that we have the blood-bought right to speak of Christianity,
humanity, morality and justice, and they cannot muzzle us, they cry "negro
equality!"

We do not desire equality with them. I hope none of us are so low and so lost to all that is noble as to wish to change places with those slave owners (all Democrats), who before the war raised men and women for the market—selling their own flesh and blood, separating husband and wife, parent and child. No, we never expect to be bad enough to be their equals. As regards color, the slave-holders did all they could to produce equality. I know many of them whose daughters in the big house were not as light as their daughters in the cabin. And when I hear the Democrats say, "Want your daughter to marry a nigger?" I tell them many of your daughters have married negroes, and many more would have done it, but you choose to sell them to white men to become victims of their lust. Shame! I say. I am tired of listening to their falsehoods, and thankful that the Chinese can rest. Last year it was Chinese and Negro; this year not one word about the "moon-eyed celestials"; and next year they will be patting you on the shoulder, saying, "Come friend, give us your vote."[3] Then should every one have the courage to say, "Depart, I never knew you, ye workers of iniquity."[4]

—Semper Fidelis.

1. Horace Greeley's Whig and then Republican newspaper, founded in 1841.
2. In her 18 October 1868 letter, published in the 23 October *Elevator*, Carter identifies this as Bath County, Kentucky.
3. Democrats were especially critical of California's large Chinese population, although even African American Republicans like Bell, who were fighting for racial equality for blacks, at times vehemently opposed Chinese suffrage (and civil rights in general), in part out of fear of competition for jobs and in part out of the same sense of xenophobia that motivated many whites. On this, see Arnold Shankman, "Black on Yellow: Afro-Americans View Chinese-Americans, 1850–1935."
4. From Matthew 7:22–23, which reads, "Many will say to me in that day, Lord, Lord, have we not prophesied in thy name? And in thy name have cast out devils? And in thy name done many wonderful works? And then I will profess unto them, I never knew you: depart from me, ye that work iniquity."

Elevator 9 October 1868: 2

Introductory to Miss Fanny Yates' Album[1]

Awake my soul! harmonious flow my muse!
To friends invite, for others to peruse;

This album waits fine pieces to receive—
Its owner thus your friendship will believe.
Your subject should be pleasing to her mind,
All written fair, with sweetest strains combin'd;
Let not your words seem harsh, or thoughts impure,—
For that will spoil, and this contempt procure;
But let your muse in sweet expressions flow,
Your secret praise in language rich bestow;
Let all your thoughts, "illum'd with fluid gold,"[2]
Possess a lustre charming to behold;
In all your words let naught be said in vain
But flow your muse in sweet celestial strain:
For know your lines are for a female's view,—
Then guard the pen, and purity pursue;
Within your mind select a pleasant theme—
The blooming rose—a soothing midnight dream;
For sweet will seem the words of every friend,
Her time your lines to read she oft will spend.
Come, write in sweetness,—banish human woes,
And this will give the owner sweet repose.

                                        —Semper Fidelis.

1. Frances Yates was the youngest daughter of William H. Yates (1816–1868), a powerhouse within San Francisco's black community. Born into slavery in the Washington, D. C./Alexandria, Virginia area, William Yates eventually bought his freedom. He worked as a porter at the U.S. Supreme Court between 1837 and 1842 and gained a rich knowledge of politics and law from overheard conversations. He is said to have worked with the Underground Railroad before moving New York City c. 1849, where he worked in restaurants, and then to California c. 1851, where his experience and refinement led to a job as a steamboat steward. He bought real estate with his earnings and rose to prominence quickly, including the presidency of the 1855 California State Convention of Colored Citizens. Douglas Daniels, who discusses Yates briefly in his *Pioneer Urbanites*, says that Yates was the *Elevator* columnist "Amego," whose work often appeared beside Carter's. See also Lapp, *Blacks in Gold Rush California*. Yates died just before this poem was published, and the album was probably a tool adults gave the nine year-old girl to cope with her loss—to "banish human woes"—and capture the sentiments of friends. Though such albums were common among literate classes, only a handful of African American albums survive. The most notable are the Amy Cassey album (the album of the wife of abolitionist Joseph Cassey and mother of Phoenixonian Institute founder Peter Cassey, which includes entries from, among others, Frederick Douglass and William Lloyd Garrison and fine watercolors by Sarah Mapps Douglass) and the albums of Mary Ann and Martina Dickerson, all currently held by the Library Company of Philadelphia.

2. This quote is drawn from the "Prologue to Mallet's Mustapha" by Scottish poet James Thompson (1700–1748).

⌒

Elevator 23 October 1868: 2
Letter from Nevada County.
Mud Hill, Oct. 18, 1868

Mr. Editor:—I do not know whether politics is the all-absorbing topic of conversation in your city, but I do know that I asked Mr. Trask how many chickens we had, and he told me "from twelve to twenty thousand majority."[1] I know we have only a few over a dozen.

Last week a lady called to see me, and we were discussing the fashions, of course. She said she would wear what she had until after election, and if Grant was not elected she would never want anything more to wear, for she would die.

I was walking on the street, and a little chap, not more than six years old, asked me who I was for. I told him I was a woman, and for nobody. He cried out, earnestly: "I thought I would find you out! You are for Seymour; all the nobodies are." I thought the little fellow was nearly right, when I saw the Democratic procession, on Friday night, in Nevada City, and listened to their Col. Larrabee.[2] A person to carry a torch in that crowd must be lost to all self-respect—must be "a nobody," even if Tom Findley was one of the Marshals.[3]

Of the intelligence of the Democrats, I will give one fact. Larrabee said lying sheets had been thrown around the county, claiming eighteen thousand majority for the Radicals in Pennsylvania. Then you ought to have heard the cheers. Poor fellows! they thought the majority he was talking about was for them. They fired guns in honor of the great Democratic "victory" in Indiana, and those "nobodies" who listened to Colonel Larrabee will not know until after Grant is President that they were firing over their own defeat.

The Democrats have circulated the report that Mr. William Mulford, of New Orleans, was one of their party, while his election as Sergeant at Arms of the Senate of Louisiana is a grand refutation of their falsehood, and gives his many friends on this coast great pleasure.[4]

One of our dailies says: "The *Examiner* claims a Mud Hill correspondent. Our editor would like to know how many votes will be polled 'at Mud Hill?'" I will tell them, none this year.[5]

A Democrat said my articles were just made-up sketches, or I would give the real names of persons and places for their benefit. I will say the Rev. Mr. B____, mentioned in my article of September 2d, was Bingham, and the place Fayetteville, Miss.; and in the next article, the B____ county was Bath county, Kentucky.[6]

I heard a Democrat on the stand here say Mr. Breckenridge was not in favor of secession until after the election of Mr. Lincoln.[7] I heard Mr. Breckenridge, in September, 1860, at Owensville, the county seat of Bath county, Kentucky, at a political meeting, where he was the principal speaker, say: "If Lincoln is elected, I say to the slave States secede." A Douglas Democrat asked him the question.[8] He hesitated for a moment, and then answered as I have written, and told the people the fact that Lincoln was an Abolitionist and the slaves would be liberated, though Mr. Lincoln did not dream of that result, because he did not expect the thing to be brought about by secession, as was advised by Mr. Breckenridge.

—Semper Fidelis.

1. "Mr. Trask," of course, is referring to potential vote counts, and, more broadly, to the presidential election of 1868, which pitted Republican Ulysses S. Grant against Democrat Horatio Seymour in a battle many saw as a defining moment as to how Reconstruction would be pursued. The vast majority of African American activists—including Bell and Carter—were ardent Grant supporters; one of the Seymour campaign slogans was "This is a White Man's County: Let White Men Rule."

2. Charles Hathaway Larrabee (1820–1883), a former Democrat congressman from Wisconsin and Civil War veteran who moved to California in 1864, practiced law in the San Bernadino area, and remained active in the Democratic party.

3. A Nevada County banker, former state treasurer (1858–1862), and active Democrat.

4. Although not mentioned in most histories of Louisiana Reconstruction, Mulford (c. 1815–?) was indeed sergeant-at-arms for the state senate; see 1870 Census of New Orleans County, Louisiana, 673.

5. The San Francisco *Examiner* was a fiercely Democratic party paper. I have found no letters from "Mud Hill" in the September and October 1868 issues of the paper, although they did have a semi-regular (and strongly Democrat) correspondent from Grass Valley, as well as a correspondent "Yuba" who reported—in deeply racist terms—on African Americans and politics (mainly from New Orleans).

6. Carter speaks of her letters of 12 September 1868 published in the 25 September *Elevator* and 2 September published in the 11 September *Elevator*.

7. John Cabell Breckinridge (1821–1875), former Kentucky congressman and vice president under James Buchanan, was nominated for the presidency in 1860 by a group of southern Democrats who walked out of the Democratic Party Convention; he was trounced by Lincoln in the election.

8. "Douglas Democrats" were the (mainly northern) members of the Democratic Party who
   eventually nominated and supported Illinois Senator Stephen A. Douglas (1813–1861) after
   the walkout noted above.

~

Elevator 13 November 1868: 2
Mud Hill, November 1, 1868

Mr. Editor:—A friend told me the world was shaking.[1] I believe it is, not
only the physical world, but the mental world. There never was a time when
mind was so agitated as the present, not only in this continent, but the Old
World is shaken. Witness the revolution in Spain.[2] Human bondage soon
will exist only in history, and religious intolerance be a dream of the past,
and mind will constitute manhood, not physical types or color of skin. And
happy are they who live in this agitation, and assist in its development! How
strange that great lessons of truth must be forced upon the mind by error
as the contrast, and a startling wrong perpetrated to ensure right, and a
long lethargic sleep to produce a full awakening! After centuries of human
bondage, man begins to realize the fact that his brother man has rights; and
this great lesson of truth is brought about by agitation, and an awakening
of mind such as the world has not seen since the Creation's dawn. In view
of this great problem being solved on both continents, what are we, as people, doing? Are we advancing to a higher civilization? or, are we standing
still? or, are we retrograding? Life is real, and an earnestness is required of
each and every one. Are we earnestly supporting institutions of learning, or
letting them die in our midst? Do we strive to cope with those around us
intellectually, or merely seek similarity in dress and carriage? Oh, if we only
knew what weight we individually carry, it does seem to me we would strive
to make a record that would tell to future ages that we struggled in this
"shaking"—that we were sincere. For words will not avail; it is acts. Let each
one bear in mind that any great enterprise by our people calls for united aid;
and whether or not we each are assigned posts of honor, let us press on, not
withdraw, through selfishness, and if we cannot, any of us, edit a readable
paper, let us unitedly assist Mr. Bell.

—Semper Fidelis.

1. San Francisco had a major earthquake on 18 October 1868.
2. In what began as a military overthrow of Queen Isabella II., the Spanish Revolution of 1868 led to universal male suffrage and some press freedoms.

⌒

Elevator, 25 December 1868: 2
Mud Hill, December 12, 1868.

Mr. Editor.—"Six feet two inches"; so said Mr. Trask to an inquiry in regard to his height. I told him I thought he was mistaken; he said not, for he was measured, and had his measurement recorded at Harper's Ferry in the summer of '51, as he was returning from Sulphur Springs, Va., where he had been for several weeks with the other members of Frank Johnson's band.[1] Judge his indignation when he arrived at Harper's Ferry; he was asked who he belonged to, if he had any scars upon him, and then measured, and told he would have to stay over night as no colored person could travel after 4 o'clock P.M.[2] He stood up, and in his wrath I guess he was six feet three inches, he pronounced curses on that State. They then threatened him with the lash, and he told them to proceed, that the first one who laid hands on him should die. And their courage was no greater then than years after, when John Brown, with a handful of men frightened the whole State,[3] for they told Mr. Trask, they knew he was a free nigger, he was so independent; and they have long ere this suffered all the curses Mr. Trask pronounced upon them, and I do not believe even the record of Mr. Trask's height could be found there now, and probably the man who wrote it down has forgotten the fact, but not forgotten is the indignity Mr. Trask suffered. Born free, living in Philadelphia, associating with men and women, respected as a gentleman, the insult will *never* be forgotten. And when anyone asks him his height he will say six feet two inches, and think of that occurance.

—Semper Fidelis

1. See the introduction of this volume. Johnson's band toured internationally, including some engagements in the upper South (especially at tourist spots). For an introduction to Johnson, see Andy Gensler, "Frank Johnson."
2. Such regulation of free blacks was common throughout the South. Indeed, approaches to "registering" free blacks in states like Virginia had, by the 1850s, become models for much of the South. The Dexter Tiffany Papers at the Missouri Historical Society,

for example, contain a "List of Free Negroes" in St. Louis c. 1850 that lists heights and occupations and includes, among others, the names of authors Lucy Delaney and Elizabeth Keckley.

3. Carter refers to John Brown's 1859 raid on the Federal Arsenal at Harper's Ferry, in which, after briefly holding the arsenal, most of Brown's party was killed by Federal troops led by Robert E. Lee. Brown was captured, hung, demonized by the South, and canonized by abolitionists. Among the myriad texts that discuss this subject, David S. Reynolds's *John Brown, Abolitionist* provides perhaps the best introduction.

⌒

Elevator 18 December 1868: 2
Mud Hill, Dec. 10, 1868

Mr. Editor,—I scarcely pick up a paper but my eyes light upon a caution to men, warning them to beware of fast women, and portraying them in hideous colors: and equally hideous to my mind, are fast men, and more to be feared than fast women—for there are ten reckless men to one bad woman the world over. I am heartedly weary of hearing my own sex derided, scoffed at—an error on the part of one person called a "general rule." A woman dares not do a righteous act without being held up to the world's ridicule, as is the case with the Minister's wife at Petaluma, who refuses the money of the Life Insurance Company.[1] They would have her accept the money and keep silent. I think she was reared by honest parents, and in childhood read often the case of Annanias and Sap[p]hira mentioned in the New Testament[2]; and as she was a woman and not a man did not want what was not legally hers—and instead of her husband's spirit coming to condemn the act, it will applaud her for her moral courage which many men will know nothing of until it is too late to mend. There are some men who cannot think or speak with respect of any woman. I say to all women beware of them, their own conduct furnishes the criterion of judgment—they are not to be trusted; and when I hear a man condemning or speaking lightly of a wo-men's character, I set him down at once as utterly devoid of virtue—search his records, and you will find it dotted with bad acts, so bad, that you wonder he had not forgotten the very word "virtue." In this day and age, women dare not treat some men with civility, for they will at once say her style is too easy, and take the liberty to insult her by language not refined. I say to women beware of men who have a low estimate of women in general. They [who] are not good sons make bad husbands and worse fathers.

—Semper Fidelis.

1. I have not yet identified this incident.
2. Acts 5 tells the story of Annanias and Sapphira, who sold a piece of land, gave part of the proceeds to the Apostles, told them they were giving them the full proceeds, and were struck dead—assumedly because of their lying.

———

Elevator 15 January 1869: 3
Mud Hill, Jan. 8, 1869.

Mr. Editor.—Nothing can be more pleasant than a ride from Nevada City to Colfax in pleasant weather, and nothing more uncomfortable than that drive of twelve miles at this season of the year, but it was resolved to celebrate the 1st in the City of Sacramento, and a few patriotic ones determined to brave wind and rain and accompany the band, whose services the Sacramentans had secured for the occasion.[1] Be it known to all who visit our city that the coaches are strong, carrying the complement inside and a deck load on the outside, and though the coach will creak like a ship in a storm and sometimes nearly overturns, never fear, Johnny Royce, our driver, is as good a Jehu as ever handled whip and reins, he will see that you are in time for the cars, and allow you to stop and drink at that beautiful fountain at the half-way house, whose three sides are enclosed, the broad side open to the street, displaying pies, cakes, huge loaves of bread, and what the male part of our company called "smiles," (and to me a misnomer—better call it tears).[2] From the half-way house to Colfax the scenery is unsurpassed, and would please the eye of the artist. Bear river and the road winding up the hills like the old Roman Labyrinth, has but one beginning and one ending, no chance to turn on cross roads, but a succession of corners turned, this a little higher than the last, and so we have reached the top. You can look back and see Bear river like a small streak of silver, and the road just passed like a long serpent. Colfax is a small place, its chief beauty is its name, yet it is a place of importance to us Nevadians as the depot for our county, our nearest approach to the Pacific Railroad, that great guide of civilization, and

when carried over that road by the iron horse and contemplating the greatness of its structure who does not have a heart full of gratitude to the Father
of Mercies that they have been permitted to live in this age, "when the faith
that removeth mountains hath entered the heart of man."[3] Many beautiful towns dot the line of the road from Colfax to Sacramento, all of them
the centres of civilization to their inhabitants—all containing some happy
homes, if you can judge from the exterior, and some aching hearts too, to
be read from the signs where they dispense "smiles;" for the prosperity of a
town cannot be known by the number of saloons, or the number of the fre-
quenters to be found at the bar drinking. While many are "smiling" there, in
lonely homes sit women and children in tears. Heaven hasten the day when
Temperance shall be triumphant.

In Sacramento, some of the company (thinking of our Granite mountains left behind,) said "What a sea of mud." Not so thought I, but what
a city of "ants;" how they labored through the floods and flames, and made
their "hills" on the low plains, and oh the dirt they have carried, load after
load, until they can say to the waters, "Thus far shalt thou go and no farther."[4] I can compare them to the coral insect who commenced his work
under water and toiled on year after year, century after century, until at last
a beautiful island rose from the depths of the sea. And so they labored on
through all discouragements, being weak, yet fainting not by the way; and
they have their reward, a beautiful city above the floods. And how it would
gladden the hearts of their ancestors in Eastern homes to see the beautiful
gardens as I saw them on the 1st day of January, 1869, filled with rose bushes
in full bloom. Of the public spirit there we have assurances that it pervades
all hearts, for the turnout to celebrate the Emancipation Act, was full evidence that the day with its halo of glories, "Freedom forever," could make
mud, rain, existing realities, nothing but straws. The Grant Guards showed
a true soldierly spirit, excellent drill, and are a fine looking set of fellows.[5]
I must give Sacramento the praise for good order. One could set in the hall
during the exercises and hear every word from the speaker's stand. The orator, Robert H. Small,[6] where has he been all these years and what doing that
we have not heard from him before? His oration was masterly, eloquent, and
pointed in *ideas*, and delivered with good elocution; it was to me a rare treat,
and I think all appreciated it, from the rousing cheers which were given frequently during its delivery. In referring to the departed Lincoln and Baker[7]
someone called out for "Tigers," which I thought was out of place. No—
tigers for the dead, rather an uplifted heart, and bowed head. Mr. Bell, you

ought to have been there to enjoy all the good things. Hospitality reigned supreme. Mr. Williams and lady deserve mention as having one of the finest lunches on record, and partaken of by hundreds I met for the first time.[8] Mr. Basil Campbell and wife of Cache Creek, Mr. Duplex of Marysville, dear friends of Mr. Trask for many long years, and I hope to call them mine from this time on.[9] I stopped with your tried friends, the Harpers[10]; you know as well as myself their hospitality—nothing better this side of heaven. Of the music I shall not say much, for all who heard it pronounced it good. The committee being earnest workers they kept the band at work. Our thanks are due the President and all the officers of the Pacific Rail Road Company for their kindness shown, and in pleasant weather we will turn out strong and give them a benefit. We hope to see the day soon, when we can welcome the many dear friends to our city and make some return for their kindness.

—Yours, Semper Fidelis

1. Nevada City residents going to Sacramento would often ride via coach or wagon to Colfax, where they could catch a train for the remainder of their journey. Carter here describes attending Sacramento's 1 January 1869 Emancipation celebration.
2. I have not yet identified Johnny Royce. "Jehu" refers to one of the Kings of Israel who was famed for his chariot-driving; see 2 Kings 9 and 10. The "smiles" are, of course, alcohol.
3. A variation of 1 Corinthians 13:1–2, "Though I speak with the tongues of men and of angels, and have not charity, I am become as sounding brass, or a tinkling cymbal. And though I have the gift of prophecy, and understand all mysteries, and all knowledge; and though I have all faith, so that I could remove mountains, and have not charity, I am nothing."
4. A variation of Job 38:11, in which God describes how he walled in the world's oceans.
5. The Grant Guards were a Sacramento black drill/social organization who shared their name with several other militia groups.
6. Not to be confused with black South Carolina Congressman Robert Smalls, Robert H. Small was a successful black miner and activist about whom little biographical information is available. See Beasley, *Negro Trail Blazers*.
7. Abraham Lincoln and friend Edward Dickinson Baker (1811–1861). Baker served as an Illinois congressman before moving to San Francisco in 1851. Though he left California for Oregon in 1860 (and served as a U.S. senator from Oregon), he raised a regiment for the Union made up largely of Californians and, after he was killed in the Battle of Ball's Bluff, was buried in San Francisco. See Gayle Anderson, "The Public Career of Edward Dickinson Baker."
8. Probably James Williams (1825–after 1873), a fugitive slave who became active in the Underground Railroad in Pennsylvania and Massachusetts before moving to California in 1851. A Sacramento resident (miner, wagon driver, merchant, and restaurant owner) since c. 1854, he participated in the rescue of fugitive slave Archy Lee and was active in the A.M.E. Church. His narrative, *The Life and Adventures of James Williams*, was published in Sacramento in 1873.
9. Basil Campbell was born a slave in Missouri in 1823 and, after several sales, was brought to California in 1853. He and his owner agreed that he would be freed after ten years of work;

in 1861, though, he paid $700 to cover the rest of his "term." He was already acquiring
land and stock, and, by 1865, when he was a vice president of the California Convention of
Colored Citizens, he was a wealthy rancher and landowner. His wife, Rececca Dalton, was
from Sacramento. See *Memorial and Biographical History of Northern California*, 323–324.
Edward Park Duplex (1830–5 January 1900) trained as a barber in his native Connecticut,
came West during the Gold Rush, and established the Metropolitan Shaving Salon in
Marysville. A mine owner, correspondent of *Frederick Douglass's Paper*, and activist, Duplex
became California's first black mayor when nearby Wheatland elected him in 1888. On
Duplex, see Lapp, *Blacks in Gold Rush California*, and Beasley, *Negro Trail Blazers*.
10. Probably William H. and Emaline Harper, who are listed in the 1870 Federal Census of
Sacramento (236). This may be the same William H. Harper who owned part of the Harper
and West Hotel in San Francisco and was active in the black community there.

⌒

Elevator 5 February 1869: 2
Mud Hill, January 31, 1869

Mr. Editor:—In San Francisco you have Earthquakes, Smallpox and Veloci-
pedes, all exciting and more or less fatal.[1] Yet here we have something more
fearful than either; some few months ago a fever broke out in our city. At
first it was mild in form and did not create consternation; it attacked only
the male portion of the inhabitants. We all thought it would abate and gradually and finally die out, but for the want of thorough sanitary measures the
spread of the contagion became general, and now there is not a man in our
city but has it. So far it has baffled the skill of physicians, and I doubt if one
can be found in the whole world able to cure the afflicted with this fearful
fever. The first symptom of it is partial insanity, a desire to get away from
families or friends, a distaste for all surroundings, books, music, conversation
of wife, nursery prattle of children and everything that formerly made life
endurable now make it unbearable, and nothing can save them. When the
fever becomes firmly seated the victim will often sacrifice household goods
and break in upon the comforts of home, the furniture, bedding, and even
the bible of a dead mother—still the fever continues. At its present rate of
increase by the month of May there will be five hundred women to one man
in this city. The disconsolate faces of women, and the sad wail of fatherless
children will greet us on every hand—how fearful! To show you how this
epidemic rages, I will relate one fact: A man just attacked with the fever was
seen reading a letter to a group of seven men, and when he finished the letter

his case was past cure, and the seven men were down with the fever. Forty new cases reported from one saloon; all took the disease from one man's conversation. It is not confined to nationality: white men, colored men and China-men are alike stricken; all to go the same way. I know not how long this state of things will continue; if no more men come to our city to add new fuel to the flame, we may see the end—earthquakes, small pox, veloci-pedes are nothing to White Pine fever.[2]

—Semper Fidelis

1. "Velocipedes" refers to a range of early bicycles, which had become popular in San Francisco and would lead to pedi-cabs and rickshaws.
2. Silver ore was discovered on "Treasure Hill" in White Pine, Nevada, in late 1867, and late 1868 and early 1869 saw a massive exodus of miners from California—including a number of African Americans. The *Elevator* covered the phenomenon in some depth.

⌒

Elevator 12 February 1869: 2
Mud Hill, Feb 7, 1869.

Mr. Editor,—Bugs! Bugs!! Bugs!!! What an infliction! Last week when I chronicled the fever that was slaying all the men of the place, I did not think so soon to pour into your readers' ears a description of the Egyptian plague that has fallen on our women. I imagine I see you start and exclaim, "Bed Bugs! Poor house keepers—untidy mortals." Not so, Mr. Editor, our women are neat, tidy, good house keepers, and bed bugs are not the bugs that have turned our town "topsy turvy." It is not lady bugs, yet it seems to find a home with them. It is not striped bugs yet it acts streaked. It has ren-dered invalids of several, taken money from the pockets of others and takes the common sense of all who come in contact with it. One form the bug assumes is unlimited faith, an unbounded confidence in the skill of others. After reason has deserted its throne, there is plenty of room for the bugs to thrive and hold riot. This is apparent to all observers. In our city are people who believe that one can by charms bring back faithless lovers, or transform men who never loved, into lovers, even if they are farther away than your city, and again they believe, that they can by charms prohibit marriages, and wives consult this charm to find whether their husbands are loving and true.

People who if you were to say spiritualism[1] to them, would raise their hands in holy horror—yet they can be seen wending their way to where one dispenses these charms for money. Of the evil one person can do to another there is no limit, yet they cannot do it by charms, and truly this is one of the greatest follies for people to throw aside sense, and give up to such foolish fancies. It was told me by a lady, that a man in our city went to San Francisco, and brought home a quantity of these charms for married women, and every one he gave charms would be devoted to him. So you see it is not Bed Bugs, Lady Bugs, or Striped Bugs that are destroying us mentally and morally, but HUMBUGS.

—Semper Fidelis

1. Like many connected to the African Methodist Church, Carter was quite hesitant about spiritualism. The California black community seems to have been a bit more welcoming to a broader sense of spiritual conjuring practices, though, and papers like the *Elevator* regularly carried ads for astrologers, fortune tellers, and clairvoyants during this period.

⌒

Elevator 5 March 1869: 2

"MY AUNT SYBEL."
by Semper Fidelis

I was a very small girl when I first saw my Aunt Sybel; she was then about thirty years of age, and if I had not been told by my grandmother, I should have thought she was as old as grandma, who was then over fifty. She was a little body, so slight and frail looking, I wondered if she was not afraid of "being blown away." Her dress, to me, looked very queer. A plain black gown, cut in quaker style (grandma said) a white handkerchief neatly folded around the neck; the ends crossing the breast, pinned neatly under the arms, with a plain black muslin cap on her head, from out which peeped two black, sad eyes. I saw her every day for one week, and I never saw her smile, neither did she frown, but always the same sad expression and still, quiet way. I made up my mind she was very poor, for grandma bought a great many things for her, and they cut and made several of those queer dresses, all of which were of black cloth. One morning she left us, and when she kissed me good-bye, she said: "may you grow up, dear child, to be happy or die early." I said to grandma: "I am glad Aunt Sybel has gone, for she makes me feel like crying, and she said she wished me dead." Grandma says you call her "Crying Aunt Sybel," and when she was a child she was called sweet little Sybel, and when she grew to womanhood, everyone said 'Singing Sybel,' for her voice was as sweet as a Lark's, and almost as cheerful, from morn til night she would sing; and then she was very beautiful, it would do any one good to look upon her face; then there was no sadness; when she was sixteen she was called hand-some, happy, Sybel, and when she spoke of your dying early, I dare say, she thought of her wrecked life, for if ever a woman has known sorrow, she has. When she was sixteen years old she was married to your father's half-brother, Brown, who was then a very handsome young man, of twenty two years of age; he was a fast youth; an indulgent mother had never left a wish ungrati-fied, deeming the child of her old age too good to be corrected and so he grew up self-willed, thinking a whole world should do him homage. He was very generous, and could well afford to be, for your father's step-mother was wealthy, and when she married your grandfather she retained her own fortune, and your Uncle Brown had only to ask for money and he had it to spend as he pleased. In those days your grandfather used to keep liquors of different kinds always on the side-board and everyone drank. Temperance Societies were unknown. Your father's own brothers and himself had always drank whenever they felt like it, but somehow, they did not care much for it; not so with your Uncle Brown when an infant, and they gave him gin slings to quiet him, he would smack his little lips and cry for more, until he was so drunk he could not see; and when a lad of five or six years of age, he would drink his toddy and then clean out the glasses when others had drank. So he kept on until he was twenty—people said he could drink more rum, and not feel it, than any other man in town. I knew it was hurting him, and he did not feel it, for he could not do without it; and so did his mother, but she had not restricted him when younger, and of course, could not then. We all had hopes that your Aunt Sybel would be able to advise him, for he loved her very much, and she had such sweet, winning ways, it seemed impossible to resist her. I think he tried to not let her see him drunk when they were first married, for she told your grandmother that he did not drink as much as she thought he did by the way people talked to her. His mother built him a pretty cottage on the banks of the Hudson river. (The same you saw last year when we were North—Mrs. Newcomb[1] lives in it.) It was furnished throughout. About the time your grandfather died he left his property to the children of his first wife, and the old homestead was sold. Your grandmother then went to live with your Uncle Brown. She built a Cotton mill, and he was overseer of the mill.

"Three years after they were married, your Uncle Brown, and his wife and baby visited me here. He came to purchase a cargo of cotton, to manufacture into cloth. The business was new then, and many people thought no good could come of spinning and weaving cloth by machinery, and wondered what women would busy themselves about when the spinning wheel and loom were put one side. Your father was supercargo for your Uncle Brown, and he told me he was drunk all the way from New York to New Orleans, and at one time threatened to kill him for some imaginary affront, he succeeded in eluding Brown, until they could secure him.

"I tell you he tried my patience, but I tried to make everything pleasant for your Aunt Sybel, she was so different from the last time I had seen her; she did not sing for her baby, but seemed to be looking away into the future with dread. He used to feed the baby with gin-sling whenever he could get the chance, and one time I told him one drunkard in the family was enough; he answered me with an oath, that his drink cost me nothing, and after that I let him alone; and glad was I when they left; and when I kissed that dear baby, I thought as your Aunt Sybel said to you, "may you die young." They had trouble from the day that they sailed from here; he acted so bad, your father had him confined in the cabin for several days, and when he had partially sobered up they allowed him his liberty. As soon as he could he went to drinking again. Your father was sitting on the deck reading; he had his left hand laying on the bench by his side, when Brown came stealthily up to him, with a hatchet in his hand, and before your father could get out of his way he severed two of his fingers. I remember the last time you saw your father, you asked him how he lost his fingers, and he evaded answering you, for I suppose the memory was too painful. They confined him again in the cabin until three days before they arrived in New York, when he plead so hard with your Aunt Sybel for his liberty, and promised to let drink alone, she allowed him to go free. The first thing he done was to find the rum and drink until he was intoxicated, and he then seized his little boy and threw him overboard before any one could stop him, and he attempted to throw your Aunt Sybel over too, but a sailor knocked him down.

"The dear baby found an ocean grave, as he sank before the boat could reach him. Your Aunt Sybel went insane, and was for six years in a Lunatic Asylum. The cotton mill was burned; it was supposed by your Uncle

Brown's own hands in a drunken fit (although people said it was a judgment from heaven because they tried to make woman's work easier) and four years after when all his property was squandered, and he had sold even the portraits of his father and mother for rum, his body was found by the roadside, frozen to death. In seven years he had drank up eighty thousand dollars, made a cripple of your father, murdered his child, rendered insane his wife, and killed his mother through grief, and died like a dog. When your Aunt Sybel regained her reason she went to live with a Quaker uncle and aunt, and assumed their style of dress, only she has worn black, no other color. They are both dead now, and she will live with a married daughter of theirs; she is poor, and I always have helped her, and shall while I live."

Such was the history of my Aunt Sybel, given by my Grandmother, and as all are sleeping, I have written it out as a warning to parents in California to refrain from wine drinking or giving to children, for so surely the taste cultivated in childhood grows with years. In 1861 I visited Aunt Sybel's grave and I have thought much since of the inscription on her tombstone, "Sorrow on earth, rest in Heaven."[2]

1. I have not yet been able to identify Mrs. Newcomb or the other figures discussed here.
2. This epitaph addresses a range of Biblical discussions of heavenly "rest," including those in Psalms and Hebrews.

Elevator 26 March 1869: 2
Mud Hill, March 21, 1869

Mr. Editor—A very dear friend now, and a schoolmate of mine years ago, who is now a public advocate of woman rights of the most radical kind, wrote to me a letter, disapproving of my "crude and baby ideas of woman's dignified position," and she asked me, "if I could not find plenty of examples in history to censure my course and sanction hers." I have been reading of late to find my errors, and correct them if possible: but I tell you, Mr. Editor, she will have the benefit of my reading, and I hope they may prove "crumbs of comfort" to her. Two thousand years ago, lived Cornelia, daughter of Scipio Africanus the conqueror of Hannibal; she was married to Tiberius Gracchus, who died, leaving to her care twelve children.[1] She devoted herself to the care and education of her children. Plutarch says of them, that "Cornelia brought them up with so much care, that though they were without dispute of the noblest family, and had the happiest geniuses of any of the Roman youths, yet education was allowed to have contributed more to their perfections than nature." She gave public lectures on philosophy in Rome, and Cicero says "if she had not been a woman, she would have deserved the first place among philosophers." History records that the Triumvirate in want of a great sum of money to carry on a war, drew up a list of fourteen hundred of the wealthiest women of Rome, determined to tax them. The women, after having tried in vain to persuade the Triumvirate to allow them to live as before, without taxation—Chisa Hortensia accompanied her to the market place, when she addressed them, and so successful was she that the list was reduced from fourteen hundred to four hundred.

In 1172, when Ancona was besieged by the Imperial troops, Oldrude, Countess Bertinoro, addressed the soldiers; her words were received by the soldiery with great applause—the sound of trumpet and clashing of arms. The enemy alarmed at the noise fled, thinking a large force had reinforced the beseiged. Nothing given by the pen of the historian is more beautiful than the speech of Galeanna in Rome, when she went from Bologno to visit her husband whom she expected to find a Senator, instead he was in a dungeon and his life in danger. She went herself to the council, and with true eloquence did she appeal to the public faith. She saved the life of her husband by the burning words she uttered.

In the year 1808, Agostina, maid of Sargossa, by a few earnest words accompanied by her own energy aroused the men of that city to deeds of bravery, saved Sargossa to Spain and rendered her fame immortal. These examples are enough this time, and I will review them for our material benefit. The character of Cornelia is truly beautiful, taken as wife or mother. We see from her example what woman can do as educator. It seems to me I need no better proof of "my crude and baby ideas of womanhood" that the mother[']s place is teaching the child, instead of ignoring the education of the child to teach the men their duty. Cornelia gave lectures after her children had passed from her care—and though it is said she made many disciples, yet all writers agree that the great beauty of her character is shown more clearly in her sons, or as she said, "her jewels." In the address of Hortensia, she asked not for representation with taxation "but desired that they might live as before, and that they never would have appeared before them had they not made use of all other means their natural modesty could suggest. Though our appearing may seem contrary to the rules prescribed for our sex, yet the loss of fathers, children, husbands and brothers may sufficiently excuse us, especially when their unhappy deaths are made a pretence for our further misfortunes," so said Hortensia.

In Bertinoro's example there is nothing unwomanly. In the besieged city when those who had appealed to her among them were women and children, and she says—"fortified and encouraged by the favor of heaven and contrary to the customs of my sex, I have determined to address you." During the late war, women [may have] done more probably to carry it to a successful issue by their eloquence, public and private, than the combined votes of all the women in the world—and reason is the cause as in the Countess Bertinoro, they spoke through the affections not through ambition. The same can be said of Gealleanna in Rome. [The following five words were included because of a printer's or editor's error.] The life of her husband[.] [A]mbition was not the motive [,] but love. I cannot see anything in it that savors of woman's rights in the radical sense. In the maid of Sargossa, we see that a woman can accomplish when called out by extraordinary circumstances. I will write nothing more, I was referred to these examples as showing "woman's dignified position" in a truly "woman's rights" view; if I fail to see it I suppose it is owing to my "crude and babified idea of true womanhood."

—Semper Fidelis.

1. Carter's references here and throughout draw on her background as an avid reader and former teacher.

~

Elevator 9 April 1869: 2
Mud Hill, April 4, 1869

Mr. Editor,—The 30th of March being the anniversary of my birth, and having no dear friend to bake a cake for me (as in my childhood days) I bethought to myself of a region round about Mud Hill that I had not explored, and having a desire to be rich, with one eye open to quartz ledges, and the other to Nature's beauties, I started out. A little distance west of Mud Hill is a miner's cabin, situated in one of the most romantic places imaginable—sheltered between two large hills, and nearly surrounded, with one by its south side open, and a creek whose running waters made ceaseless music, from the cabin door to the bank of the creek a gentle slope, the green grass and wild flowers growing to the edge of the bank, and some of the flowers I saw, whose tops had fallen over the bank to kiss the water as it went singing by. The tall pines standing as Grant's sentinel over that cabin— the birds singing among their branches made the place seem enchanted. I set down on the threshold of the door and asked the fairies to come and bring me the occupant of the place. I had no sooner made my wish and raised my eyes, than I saw standing before me a tall feeble old man, he was so forbidding in appearance I started to withdraw, "Stay, I am powerless to harm," he said. I asked him where he came from, and as he was clothed in rags, I at once thought he was no spirit. While waiting for his answer (in true Yankee style), I asked him if he built the cabin and why he built it in such a romantic spot. Here is his story: "I came from Massachusetts in the year 1848— came to California to get rich, for I had a wife and six children, and I was tired of working day after day for just enough to live on, and when the end of the year came round, not one cent ahead. The newspapers were all filled with the golden stories, so I asked Susan (for that was my wife's name) if she could manage without me for two years (as in that time I would make my pile and go home). I would send her money so often as I got a chance. Well, I left them the cottage, five dollars and my blessing, and with five dollars more, I started, I worked my way around the Horn, and in a little over five months was in the golden land, I worked my way into the mines and the first place I mined was in this Creek, in front of the cabin; I had a tent on the same place and when the fall rains began I put up the cabin. The day I commenced it I sent a check home to Susan of one hundred and fifty dollars, and wrote to her to live well that winter and the next summer I would work out my claims and come home. After my cabin was done a fellow came along and made himself sociable like, told me he was from old Massachusetts, and offered to pay for half the cabin if I would take him in. Well, I was raised pious like, never played cards, did not know one card from another. When the long rainy days set in, the fellow brought out of his carpet bag a pack of cards, and told me he would teach me all the games he knew just for amusement; I learned fast, and the more I played the more I liked it. At home I never drank nothing stronger than cider, but this fellow would go to town and come back with Old Bourbon, and by spring, I could drink as much as he could. Well, I played cards and drank whiskey, and when the water was low enough in the Creek to go to work in the month of May I had no claim: I had gambled it away—the Massachusetts fellow had played me out of it. I went over on the Yuba[1] that summer and worked, made nothing, came back in the fall and found my Massachusetts fellow getting ready to go home: he had made six thousand dollars out of my claim, and when he went away he gave me his grub in the cabin—one sack of self rising flour, twenty pounds of beans, and some salt pork. I did not go home, did not send my wife any more money, and from that day to this I have played cards and drank whiskey. It is twenty years since I left home, and ten years since I heard from any of them, I know I shall never hear from or see them again, for whiskey has nearly done its work. I like this place and hope I may die here."

I shall never ask the fairies to help me again, for romance faded too quick into reality so stern and forbidding, that the beautiful spot seems no longer beautiful.

—Semper Fidelis.

P.S.—How sorry I was that the fairy did not tell me a pretty tale to write with my nice new Gold Pen that your gentlemanly agent at Truckee[2] sent me, with these words: "I send you a Pen as an appreciation in part for your Elevator letters." May he be blessed, and may that pen be devoted to right.

—S.F.

1. Nevada County's parent (and neighboring) county.
2. The *Elevator*'s agent at Truckee Station was Frederick B. W. Grinage (c. 1828–?), a Maryland-born barber who lived in Placer County, California, before moving to Carson City, Nevada. See 1870 Census of Placer County, California, 459; the 1880 Census of Ormsby County, Nevada, 64D, and Rusco, *Good Time Coming*.

⁓

Elevator 30 April 1869: 2
Mud Hill, April 25, 1869

Mr. Editor,—On the street yesterday, I passed a group of little girls engaged in earnest conversation, and catching the remark of the least one, I slackened my speed to listen to them. The eldest of the group of six I judged to be about ten years of age, and the other ages varying from that down to four—and it was this little four year old who had arrested my attention by gravely saying: "my childer thall go to thunday thool." I at first thought their children spoken of were their dolls, as they had them with them, but I soon learned better and knew they were speculating of the years to come, when they should be fulfilling the duties daily performed by their mothers; and these children taught me wisdom—gave me an insight into each one of their hearts, and the hearts of their mothers. One said her children "should not play ball, because they made so much noise and woke baby up." Another said, "my little girls shall have silk dresses with two flounces on them." But it was for the eldest to change the whole current of my thoughts. Full of youthful fancy to a view of anxious, sad inquiry— "my children shall never drink whiskey." As the words passed her lips, I involuntarily turned to view the face, and I saw written there, what God never designed should mar the face of childhood—sadness—unutterable sadness! Thinking of her face and words, I stopped to call on a friend, and making some inquiries, I soon had a history common to California, but so fearful as to make it no more endurable by being an every day occurrence.—The parents of this girl came to California from Connecticut, seven years ago, both endowed with superior mental and physical constitutions, with high hopes and considerable money. They commenced a life of pleasure, business prospered, and both being very social they soon had hosts of friends around them—social parties with wine in abundance was before them, and it was not long before champagne suppers began to tell on the father. Business was neglected, a failure ensued; they then changed their location, but the habit was too firmly fixed to be affected by change, and soon poverty with its attendant ills was theirs. The mother died. The father is a confirmed drunkard, and three children are without a protector—and this is an everyday occurrence in California. If the aching, breaking and broken hearts were weighed in the same scale with the gold, the gold would fly up light as air, while the hearts would weigh down! down!! down!!!

—Semper Fidelis.

Elevator 7 May 1869: 2
Mud Hill, May 1, 1869

Mr. Editor:—I have read your earnest appeal to our people on the subject of organization, and I earnestly hope they will not let it pass unheeded.[1] An indifference at the present time betokens positive insanity. After all the wonders wrought out for us in the last seven years, the struggle of blood and treason to bring us to the river, Progress, which, if we cross, must be by our own efforts; we sit calmly down with folded hands waiting for something to turn up. We must all be aware that the 15th Amendment is the last thing that will be done for us by the so called "ruling powers," and if we remain inactive our children will curse our apathy when we are slumbering in our graves, and wonder why we did not bestir ourselves when action was so much needed, and its effects would have been so telling.[2]

I know not how it is in San Francisco, but here there is an indifference on the subject of education that is deplorable. Many who cannot read will not learn, even in view of the fact that the right of suffrage is to be theirs and that an intelligent voter is the proper one. A gentleman whose efforts have never ceased in our behalf, even in a time when to talk in favor of justice to the black man would bring persecution, told me a few days since that he was slowly losing faith in us as a people destined to stand alone—not in our ability to stand, but in our willingness. He said, "it seemed to him that we had fallen asleep when Lincoln went to his untimely grave." Is it so? Is there nothing to arouse us?

Because persecution has in a measure ceased, all our energy has left us. This time there is more need of action than at any time since the immortal Lincoln issued his Emancipation Proclamation. Let us show to the world that we appreciate all that has been done for us, by now doing for ourselves. Let us not sit quiet for fear we will make a wrong move, for if we once begin to act how soon duty's path will be plain before us. In this day and age one ought to be willing to do, dare, and even die if called upon.

We want our altars and hearths to remain a sacred legacy to our children. We want all our rights, educational, civil and religious. We want them to-day, and we want to transmit them unsullied to our children's children forever.

It has been told me that the change in this place in the last ten years has been backwards. That ten years ago there was an earnestness in all things, a desire to learn, great sacrifices made for knowledge, a unity of feeling and a desire to help one another along. Since then a going back ward, no desire for knowledge, a hatred towards those who try to make themselves useful, a spirit of envy towards those who succeed in life. This state of things cannot exist. So sure as water seeks its level will all such conduct rebound to our injury.

Mr. Editor, write, cease not, get the people in San Francisco to act, act as a unit. Will not the people there make example for the Pacific coast? Organize! Organize!! Present a united front to the enemy. Let all mankind know we are in earnest and are not to[o] lazy to progress.

—Semper Fidelis.

1. The 16 April 1869 *Elevator* carried Bell's essay "Need of Organization," which forcefully called for organized action among blacks at both the local and state levels.
2. Carter saw the Fifteenth Amendment as an important potential victory for the Civil Rights struggle, but also only a step in that struggle.

⌒

Elevator 28 May 1869: 2

MRS. TRASK ON TRAIN
Mud Hill, May 23rd, '69

Mr. Editor,—The world is on the lookout for something exciting—California is no exception to the rest of the world. The organization of mankind is in a measure changed since the days of Puritanism, for then men were content to perform weekly secular duties, and Sunday devotions, year after year, never dreaming that the great "desideratum" was within their reach. If they could only have known something of "hero-worship," in those days of "staid proceedings," how different the history that has come down to us. Well, we are a long way from them in our likes and dislikes, whether the change is for the better remains to be seen. Could we in California live without a weekly sensation—what would our editors do? Would there be any necessity for daily journals, who would read them if they did not reveal something terrible? In our associations, do we not enjoy the society of the noted, oftentimes overlooking true merit, because it is not coupled with notoriety? I am admonished every day that the exciting sensational in the literary world has full sway. Men, women and children are moved alike by something that has an existence only in a diseased imagination, while common sense is entirely overlooked. The rage for hero worship is so strong, that they will conjure up a hero that has not one characteristic worthy of worship; install him in their hearts and homes—yes, reach way down in their pockets to do him honor. All these thoughts have been brought to mind by reading the proceedings in San Francisco of that windy "Train." Is not our country full of heroes, who have faced death at the cannon's mouth, who are maimed by shot and shell, who by their actions have shown the world that they were worthy of worship? No! we pass them all by, and like many ladies worship a "Train," because, we think, it adds to our stateliness, among those by whom we are surrounded; and one sits near me who says "many things in the earth, and in the heavens" that add to their length and beauty by "Trains." The most brilliant comet would appear to us no more, than one of the stars that nightly greet our vision, if divested of its "train" of light, and the railroad worse than useless with its iron bands if it were not for the "trains" running day and night upon its rails. I say truly, and Democracy being sick might die, if it were not for the sensation hero "Train"—and the radical women's rights movement might languish, if it were not backed up and supported by that self hero George Francis Train.[1]

—Semper Fidelis.

P.S.—I know what I have written will make me "*non popularis*," and I do not care.

—S.F.

1. George Francis Train, entrepreneur and self-styled populist politician (and the basis for Phineas Fogg in Jules Verne's *Around the World in 80 Days*), made several stops in California on a national lecture tour. See notes to Carter's letter of 20 February 1868 in the 6 March 1868 *Elevator*, as well as Willis Thornton, *The Nine Lives of Citizen Train*, and the introduction to this volume.

⌒

Elevator 4 June 1869: 2–3

Two Pages of Autobiography.
Mud Hill, May 29th 1869

Thirty nine years ago might be seen standing by the side of an old tumble down building in New Orleans, two men reading a notice or advertisement of a sale to take place the next day, which notice read as follows:

"For sale, four likely negroes. One very bright mulatto woman and child. She has been waiting maid to a young lady, has travelled through

Europe, can speak three languages; she would be invaluable to any one wishing to travel, a fine chance for a single gentleman to spend money—also three plantation hands, all of which will be sold cheap."

Now these men reading did not wish to purchase, they were cousins from New York, strangers in that city, and to see a human being sold to the highest bidder, was to them something so rare, so curious, they determined to attend the sale.

The next morning, bright and early the bidding commenced. One of the men was sold first—he was struck off [for] one thousand dollars. As there seemed to be a lack of spirit among the bidders, the woman was brought out and placed on the block for all to look at: the auctioneer saying at the same time, "Look well, fellers, ain't she a fine sight, well now I tell ye, I must sell them two niggers there, 'fore I sell the gal"—and ordering the woman down another man took her place, and as the interest had increased, the sale of the two men did not occupy many minutes, when the woman with the babe in her arms stood up before that crowd of men, while the salesman cried out, "come and examine her, walk up gentlemen, and look for yerselves." Dear readers! have you never seen dear ones on the shores of time, when the veil between the visible and invisible was nearly rent in twain, when you knew they were between two worlds and both seen by their eyes? Have you never gazed on their glorified faces and read therefrom "Earth is beautiful, but Heaven is glorious?" So this woman looked to these cousins. A face of perfect beauty but white as alabaster, with eyes black as a raven, and bright, giving out of them a look so earnest that it burned into the hearts of the few true and good among the many in that crowd. The two strangers walked up with the rest and took a position near the block. The babe was crying, but it was kept covered, the mother slightly swaying it in her arms, looking as if unable for even that effort. After examining her as one would a horse, the people were called on to bid. They were told that the "gal" would be sold first, and the child afterwards. The first bid was seven hundred dollars, then one of the cousins bid eight hundred, some one bid nine hundred and the other cousin bid one thousand dollars—all the money they had between them. After that they could merely watch the others, and soon she was struck off to a man whose face bespoke villainy for eighteen hundred dollars; who when the child was uncovered for sale, and he had looked at it said "Go to Hell with the brat, I don't want to buy the plague." It was hard to get a bid for the babe, at last one man bid twenty five dollars. She then turned to the cousins and said, "Please buy my baby, you look as if you were kind and good." One of them cried out fifty dollars and the child was his. The mother said, "its father died two months ago, its name is Truey. Do right by it and may God bless you—it is only a little helpless thing eight days old. I am going where its father is." She then kissed it, watering its face with her tears, and mother and child parted never to meet until time shall end. Eight days old! Dear baby, never to know a mother's love, yet live to say, when nearly forty years of age, "I never knew a mother's devotion, my mother died when I was nine days old, I was raised and cared for by my uncle and grandmother." Yes, the next day the cousins went to see the owner of the mother, thinking to persuade him to take the child as a gift, when they learned she was dead. I may tell the readers sometime more of True Montague's life.[1]

—Semper Fidelis

1. Carter's 14 August 1869 piece in the 20 August 1869 *Elevator* offers another story of True Montague. She also mentioned working on a larger version of the story in her 29 June 1870 letter, published in the 8 July 1870 *Elevator*. Some of the similarities to events described in her earlier *Elevator* work certainly would have suggested to readers that True Montague's story might have been partially autobiographical—or, at least, the story of a close friend.

Elevator 25 June 1869: 2
Oroville, June 13th, 1869

Mr. Editor,—California as a part of Uncle Sam's domains is truly an important part, and that she will furnish homes for thousands of Europe's poor, Asia's industrious and Africa's once despised is a thing only of days. To know the greatness of our state one must travel its length and breadth, visit its mountains and valleys, hills and plains. California embraces all climates; it has regions of perpetual summer, and Sierras where eternal winter reigns; fields ever bright with perennial green, and forests always glowing in Autumnal beauty. Oroville,[1] the country seat of Butte County, is a pleasantly located town, connected by Railroad with Maryville, and of course, easy of access to San Francisco, the city of cities of California. From Maryville here is one continuous plain, a level country sparsely settled although a great part of the land is under cultivation, but I should think from what I saw not properly cultivated. The neatness and thrift of New England farming is entirely overlooked. The money making, an ever restless feeling that actuates people of every pursuit in California is a great drawback to the prosperity of the country. When farmers come to California to remain permanently, purchase small farms, build good houses and barns, substantial fences, set out plenty of fruit and ornamental trees, adding year by year improvements, having schoolhouses easy of access, churches within reasonable distances: then will this state surpass every other in the Union.

That the people of Oroville are imbued with taste is manifest in the improvements made, the regularity of the Streets—the comfortable houses and yards full of fruit trees and flowers. I think I have seen no prettier place in California for a home than Oroville. It is a mining town, but surrounded by land fit for agriculture, which argues well for the continued prosperity of the place. I learn there are some very wealthy men in this place, but are unwilling to spend their money here: I suppose like the most of Californians preferring "to go home"—but many of them will, like "Obidah, son of Abensina, die in Bagdad,"[2] viz—California; Oroville gave forty nine Republican majority out of a little over four hundred votes polled. There are very few colored people living here. They all speak in terms of highest praise of Rev. Mr. Bates[3] the Methodist Minister, who is without prejudice regarding color. God has some true and good men left on this earth, and when we see one taking public opinion, throwing it on one side, when it comes in contact with duty it keeps our faith in humanity. The local paper is what I call an itemized journal,[4] having two columns of small items in each week's issue, the collecting of which must employ the brain of one man. I suppose it is a good paper, and answers the people for an advertizing [sic] medium. Its politics are doubtful, and yet it is not neutral. I think the Apostle's words addressed to one of the churches in Asia, applicable to the Butte *Record*, "because you are neither cold or hot, I will spew you out of my mouth."[5]

—Semper Fidelis.

---

1. Oroville is now the town of Oro. The 1870 census lists only about three hundred residents—though the county it served was much larger. While the census lists almost eighty black residents in Butte County, it lists no black residents of Oro.

2. From Samuel Johnson's "Obidah and the hermit, an Eastern Story" in *Rambler* #65—a story
   and sentiment regularly quoted in the nineteenth century, including in schoolbooks like
   McGuffey's Fifth Eclectic Reader.
3. I have not yet located the Rev. Bates.
4. The Butte *Record*, noted later in the letter.
5. Revelation 3:16. The verse begins "So then because thou art lukewarm. . . ."

⁓

Elevator 16 July 1869: 3
Mud Hill, July 4, 1869

Mr. Editor,—Marysville has a public school for colored children, and it is
taught by Miss Florence Hatch, who is employed by the Board of Educa-
tion.¹ The school-room used is the basement of the Baptist Church.² While
in Marysville, I visited the school and counted 22 children in attendance.
Miss Hatch informed me that 29 were enrolled on the register. I heard a few
of the children read, and not being acquainted with their previous scholarship, could not judge of the progress made. I heard some of the parents
say, their children were improving, and the teacher said some of them made
rapid progress. While sitting in school one hour I wondered if teacher and
children were not ready to go home and stay, to get away from confusion
and noise. The school furniture is a disgrace to Marysville—to the Board of
Education a burning shame. One would hardly think in all the city so many
old *clap-trap*, broken down desks and benches could be found as are in that
school room. Not a child could move, but the creaks and groans would
respond to the movement. I would not teach two hours there unless the
room was newly furnished. Some of the children sitting on seats without any
backs to them, and so high from the floor, their little feet dangling, unable
to touch the tips of their toes.

In Nevada City, although the colored children have to take the old
schoolhouse,³ yet they have it furnished with patent desks just the same as the
white school, and I can see no earthly reason why the colored school in Marysville cannot have something comfortable at least. Let me impress upon parents the necessity of visiting the schools often. The children will then become
accustomed to strange faces, and will be able to pursue their studies and

recite without so much embarrassment. It is also encouraging to the Teacher to have the parents interested, and in no way can they show more interest than by visiting the school often.

—Semper Fidelis

1. Marysville, in Yuba County (next to Nevada County) had a small black population at this point (only forty-one out of over five thousand total residents in the 1870 census), but that population—once larger—still included key figures in the state like Edward Duplex and Reverend James H. Hubbard. The only "Miss Florence Hatch" I have been able to locate in Marysville was the daughter of white lawyer Francis L. Hatch; she was born c. 1851 and may well have taught briefly at the Marysville black school, as many black schools had white teachers. On Hatch, see 1860 Census of Yuba County, California, 855.
2. Probably Mount Olivet Baptist Church, which was founded in 1856, built a brick church on Sixth Street in Marysville in 1857, and was active in the 1860s and 1870s.
3. When a new school was built for white children in Nevada County, area black children "inherited" the old building.

⌒

Elevator 30 July 1869: 3

MRS. COURTNEY'S LECTURE TO HER HUSBAND
ON ELECTION DAY
Mud Hill, July 23d.

I shall vote, Courtney, if you have to stay at home with the children. Can't help it if you have to stay at home with the children. Can't help it if Jamie and Joe have the measles—children had them before and lived through it. Can't get any one to stay with them. All the women, girls and men are going to vote. I asked Mrs. Jones just to stay one hour. She said no; she must be on hand to distribute tickets and electioneer. She thanked God she had no children to be sick with measels on election day. She has been target shooting for a long time. She took her revolver with her to-day, and if necessary she says she will use it. I shall vote. Mrs. Jones said the ballot and bullet went together. She told me to come, if you staid at home. Yes, every woman must turn out, to let men know that they appreciate their privileges, and it is a "struggle for life." Miss Dickenson[1] said so.

I know my mother did not vote. She did not comprehend this "struggle." I know she was a good woman. I shall vote, Courtney. I know a man's vote is good, but a woman's is better, and it is unusual, sensational. I shall go, if the children do cry. I thank the Lord I live in a progressive age. What if I don't understand law? I know who I am going to vote for. Yes, he is a gentleman. Yes, he *has* got lovely eyes. Yes, they look melting. Yes, he talks pathetic. Yes, he opened my eyes to see all the wrong heaped upon me by denying me the right of the ballot, and giving it to those horrible negroes at the South.[2] Oh, how he suffered in prison. "In prison for horse stealing?" Aint you ashamed, Courtney, to insinuate such a thing. No, for opinion sake, in Old England. I will vote. I did not marry you to stay at home all the time. Talk as much as you please, I will vote; it is my duty. I will vote. It is a blood-bought privilege.—Well, what if women didn't fight, they can vote. Yes, we just want to show men who is ahead now. Wont be kept down a day longer. Yes, I will wear a green dress. What if I didn't come from Ireland. Mr. Train[3] loves the Irish, and believes in "wearing of the green" Yes, I know the milkmaid's soliloquy. Shan't cry over defeat. I shall vote. We will elect our man. You can wash the dishes, sweep the floor, wash the children, give them their medicine, keep the flies off them, give Jamie toast water to drink, and keep Joe covered.[4] Be sure and give the medicine right. Can't remember half I have to think of, and my country's good is the bargain. I shall vote. She who refuses would be recreant to her country's trust. No! that trust did not mean children.—Peril my children' lives by leaving them. I give all to my country. I shall vote. I shall vote. I shall vote.

—Semper Fidelis.

1. Probably a reference to Anna E. Dickinson (1842–1932), lecturer and writer, who gave her first public speeches while still a teenager and lectured throughout the 1860s and 1870s on abolition and especially women's rights.
2. A claim common in the Anthony/Stanton/Train arguments against the Fifteenth Amendment and for white women's suffrage.
3. After the partnership with Anthony and Stanton that drew Carter's ire, Train served jail time in Great Britain before returning to lecture in the U.S. (including California). See also notes to Carter's letters of 20 February 1868 published in the 6 March 1868 *Elevator* and 23 May 1869 published in the 28 May 1869 *Elevator*, as well as the introduction to this volume.
4. Common nineteenth-century mothers' work. Toast water was made by pouring boiling water over toasted bread, and then cooling the water and giving it to the patient.

Elevator 20 August 1869: 3

ANOTHER PAGE OF AUTOBIOGRAPHY[1]
Mud Hill, August 14, '69.

Mr. Editor,—In the city of Troy, New York, died a few years ago a colored woman named Deyon, aged one hundred and four years. All her years were devoted to active industry. She lived to rear four generations of children, and saw all of two and a part of the third generation consigned to the tomb, while she was little past her threescore and ten years. A slave while slavery had an existence in the State of New York, and when freedom was announced she determined to remain with the same family, and with them she continued until a few years before her death, when she lived with her descendants, but was held in loving remembrance by the many, many descendants of those for whom she had toiled in former years.[2] She raised two large families of motherless children, and to them her living words, her unceasing care and untold patience were engraved on their hearts. They and their children and children's children, never forgot the dear loving, "Mama Yonna." It was the good fortune of Tru Montague to fall into her hands in her infancy and in her childhood to spare her love, for the father of Truey was one of the children she had raised and was not dead, as her mother supposed, when she died, but had failed to reach the home awaiting him, and the heart breaking for his absence; and the poor aching heart died, believing him dead as had been told her, and when after three months he came to New Orleans to take her away forever; she had crossed the silent river and his child had been sold, and he knew not where it was. Then appeared this advertisement, "$500 reward for information of the child bought, etc." After a short time he found his child, and then his anxiety to remain forever from the possibility of being sold again he determined to take her North and commit her to the care of his grandmother. So this little waif took her first sea voyage before she was six months old, and in less than three months of feasting on Yonna's love and care was taken back to New Orleans by her father and grandmother. True's father was engaged in business that required his presence at the South a part of the time, and he was never long at home, but his affection was cent[e]red on his little affectionate daughter, who did not inherit her mother's beauty, neither her bonds, but a short time with her mother's ways she had had her father's face, and when a little more than two years old she was taken by the grandmother. The only thing left in her recollection of that visit is "Mamma Yonna" feeding Truey on "Dough Nuts"—and no one since has never been able to make them suit her taste—no one could make them like "Mamma Yonna."

—Semper Fidelis

1. True Montague's autobiography was introduced to *Elevator* readers in Carter's 29 May 1869 letter in the 4 June 1869 *Elevator*. It is briefly mentioned in Carter's 29 June 1870 letter published in the 9 July 1870 *Elevator*. As in her earlier piece on True Montague, this narrative's discussion—especially of the father and grandmother vis-à-vis New Orleans— sounds (at least partially) autobiographical.
2. New York passed a gradual emancipation law in 1799 and a stronger Abolition Act in 1817 designed to rid the state of slavery by 1827; still, a handful of New York residents remained slaves into the mid-century. Leslie M. Harris, *In the Shadow of Slavery: African Americans in New York City, 1626–1863*, provides a useful introduction, though, as its subtitle notes, it focuses on New York City.

Elevator 27 August 1869: 2
Mud Hill, August 21, '69

Mr. Editor,—Did you ever come across people who had no time to accomplish anything in life?—who were always in a hurry and yet always tangled up: and have you not felt sorry for them and would gladly have helped them out? I have seen many of that sort of people, and I knew improvement with them was impossible, yet I have felt for the children who must grow up in such a "harum-scarum" influence and be sufferers all their lives for the want of a little order. Many persons imagine good order suggestive of little comfort, and often you hear them say "too nice for comfort," "regular old maid," etc. You know Mr. Editor, mixed type is not convenient for the printer, and I know confusion is not good for the housekeeper. How easy it is to instil[l] order in the minds of children, and as soon as the little tottler [sic] can take things out of place he can be taught to replace them. As the child grows older let him understand there is a place for his things, and see that it is not occupied by any one else. When old enough to go to school, and he comes in the house, let him not throw hat or cap on chair or floor, but directly hang it in the place assigned him, and my word for it in a short time that boy will dislike disorder, as much as any "old maid."

My books are my fortune (small fortune it is too) and I treat them as dear friends, use them kindly—don't I hate to see them misused. When used I loved to see them restored to the bookcase, and in their proper places. Children should never be allowed to handle valuable books to look at engravings. I have had ladies who visited me with small children get my books of engravings to quiet their children when restless, and when I would remonstrate say, "Don't cry darling, aunty is an old maid." My grandmother taught me in childhood never to lay aside my shawl without folding, and the habit has staid by me until now. The keeping [of] responsibility from children is bad, let them understand that they must do for themselves—praise them for well doing and they will desire to be industrious and orderly.

—Semper Fidelis.

Elevator 5 November 1869: 2
Mud Hill, Oct. 27, 1869

Mr. Editor:—"What of the night?" Is there one ray of hope for California? It seems Democracy is again triumphant. When will truth prevail? Is it possible that intelligent people will be gulled by lying politicians, and men have the highest offices in the State, who, a few years ago, cursed the Government, cursed the Flag, rejoiced over every Union defeat, and went about with saddened faces when the telegraph heralded a defeat to the Confederacy? I am astonished that all this boldness (electing such men to our offices of Government) should occur so soon after great struggle, before the tears are dry for the departed heroes, who willingly went to death that the old flag might wave over a whole country with all its stars entire. There are some who can never forget those near and dear to us, who so bravely died, and never can we be reconciled to traitors, for let them talk ever so boldly of "our flag," we can look back only a few years, and then they styled it "the old rag." I wonder where consistency has fled! It surely is not with the Democratic party in California.[1]

Mr. Editor, will we not awake one of these days and hear the welcome cry of the Fifteenth Amendment[2] is an established fact? Shall we not see our men walking boldly up to the polls by that Act, saying, "I am a man in God's image, and a free man with his privileges. After all this, then may the women talk of their rights, and press the matter if they so desire."

—Semper Fidelis

1. A number of California Democrats expressed considerably pro-Southern sentiment during and after the Civil War.
2. Passed by Congress on 26 February 1869, the Fifteenth Amendment, which guaranteed black male suffrage, was finally ratified by a sufficient number of states on 3 February 1870.

⌒

Elevator 3 December 1869: 2
Mud Hill, Nov. 21, '69.

Mr. Editor,—I had company last week, and my lady visitor was from New Orleans, where she had lived seventeen years, and this is what she said to me: "I am fearful the colored people will never be as happy again as they were before the war. I used to go out to a plantation belonging to my uncle to spend Christmas week; and the colored folks had such a nice time, I used to envy them their happiness; with the turkey dinner in the day time, and their dances in the night; and my aunt had to pay one of the girls to have anything done in the house."

Mrs. Storms[1] and myself had (after the fashion of men and women also) allowed our conversation to drift on politics. Living as long as she had in New Orleans, she thought she had seen the worst of slavery. I told her that her experience was very happy indeed, but I thought one week of fifty two would hardly (let the enjoyment be ever so much) suffice for her; for there followed after, fifty one weeks of unceasing toil, oftentimes accompanied by hunger, blows and sufferings not nameable; and as she had given me so beautiful a description of Christmas week,[2] I would give her one of the weeks after, and every word true.

In 1860, in Bath Co., Ky., was a woman by the name of Hawkins, who had five slaves.[3] Near her lived a married daughter, and to her she gave one of the women, who was also the mother of three small children. Her new master was a shiftless, good-for-nothing fellow, a fair specimen of "Poor White Trash," and he made up his mind to sell the woman from her children, and often threatened her. The week after Christmas, the trader came, and he bargained her for $1000—She asked permission to go to "Old Missus" to get an apron belonging to her, and walked deliberately out to a wood pile, picked up an axe, and with her left hand, cut her right hand, severing her thumb and three fingers, leaving the fourth finger half on; then went into the house, holding up her hand, all bleeding, said to the trader, "Massa, I allow you wont want me now." The bill of sale was written but not signed, and the master and trader quarrelled, and finally agreed to compromise, her owner taking half ... five hundred dollars; then they wrapped some rags around the bleeding hand, chained her legs together, drove her to a small town called Bethel[4] (by some of the most wicked people ever belonging to a church) where they called a surgeon to dress her hand, and the inhuman wretch took a carpenter's saw to take off the remaining finger—when some one remonstrated with him and asked "why he did not use a surgeon's saw," he replied, "she ought to be in hell," which called forth from the martyred woman these words: "See to it, Massa, you ain't there first." She was put in jail that night, and the next day drove South.

—Semper Fidelis.

1. I have not yet determined the identity of Mrs. Storms.
2. Southern tradition dictated slaves receive a holiday at Christmas; among the many descriptions of this phenomena, Frederick Douglass's remains the most poignant—as it reminds readers, as does Carter, that, when given, such a holiday was, at best, simply a brief release—a pressure valve—from the realities of slavery.
3. Probably Sarah T. Hawkins (c. 1796–?), who is listed in the 1860 Federal Census of Bath County (Owingsville, 179, taken mid-year) as a widow with four slaves—a woman aged thirty-seven, a man aged seventeen, a girl aged fifteen, and a boy aged thirteen—and over $9000 in real estate and personal property. She is listed with her son-in-law William J. Berry's family. See also 1850 Federal Census of Bath County, Kentucky, 101.
4. A small town in Bath County about eleven miles from Owingsville.

—————— ⌒ ——————

Elevator 24 December 1869: 2

WEARING HORNS.
A CHRISTMAS STORY FOR CHILDREN.
Mud Hill, Dec. 12, 1869.

Mr. Editor,—Many years ago, when I was a little girl I had a cousin by the name of Fred, and he was full of life, caring more for fun than anything else. He had no scruples of conscience, everything was made subservient to him to carry out his *fun*. He being four years older than myself, was disposed to lord it over me (boy-like) and always took pains when talking to me, to remind me that I was a little girl, and frequently told me of things he had done when he was a little boy, (he was only eleven years old,) before he knew everything. He had the largest and blackest eyes I ever saw, and they would expand with his stories which were of gigantic proportions. I was a ready listener to all Fred's stories, and fully believed every word he told me, and one morning, when he came down to his breakfast rather late, and said a red calf stood before his bed and would not let him get up. I told him I would go upstairs with a stick and drive the calf down. He told me "the calf would eat me up." My grandmother invited a little girl to spend Christmas with me, and she expressed great anxiety to know how Santa Claus looked. Fred told her he always wore horns—great big horns loaded with everything nice for children, like Lucie and me, and told her Santa Claus would be sure to come that evening, but we must go to bed early and go to sleep, if we wanted Santa Claus to bring us nice things. Children nowadays don't often use Bandana handkerchiefs, and many children never saw one. When I was a child, nothing was more fashionable, and Fred had become the owner of a red one which he displayed with a great deal of vanity, often asking us if we did not wish we were large enough to have such a handkerchief, and of course, we said yes. Well the day passed, and early bed time found Lucie and me anxious to go to sleep, but sleep we could not, we lay awake whispering, so that Santa Claus should not hear us wondering what he would bring us, and all at once we heard the jingling of bells—our room door opened, and Santa Claus entered wrapped in a sheet. A large pair of horns on his head filled with dolls and toys. We lay trembling, frightened terribly, while he commenced to unload his horns, filling our stockings, and while busy at work, off fell the sheet from his body, and then Lucie spoke loud, "it is Fred, for there is his red handkerchief sticking out of his pocket!"—down came the horns—false face, and oh, how we laughed, and how the romance fled from us, and poor Fred said he would burn his red handkerchief; and today he is still wearing horns while not of the same kind he wore years ago, yet they are as false; and don't think me crazy when I say people like cattle wear horns, although not always like Fred's, visible to the eye; we can feel the hook plainly, and, sometimes hear the bellowing, and then we can prepare, and ward off the thrusts; but we oftener find ourselves gored, and cannot tell from whence comes the wound, or whose horns have done the deed.

I have been recently blessed with a visit from one whom I never expected to meet on this earth again, and to the ELEVATOR, all thanks are due for a brother and sister's meeting, for thirty-three years, and my brother R.H.H. says I wear horns, and the name of them is unforgiveness, because I say I cannot respect a parent who would lavish every good thing on one child and leave another to neglect.[1]

—Semper Fidelis

1. I have yet to determine the identities of those mentioned in this piece, including R. H. H. A man signing himself R. H. H. wrote a pair of letters published in the *Pacific Appeal* in late 1872 on conditions in Los Angeles; he may have been the "Robert H. Hyers" mentioned in one of the letters; see 12 October 1872 and 2 November 1872 issues of the *Pacific Appeal*. I have been unable to determine a connection between Hyers and Carter. The *Elevator*, like many black papers, attempted to engineer reunions of separated black families and ran ads from individuals "seeking information" on relatives.

⌒

Elevator 11 February 1870: 2–3
Mud Hill, Feb. 5, 1870

Mr. Editor,—I have just read, "Georgia has ratified the Fifteenth Amendment." I can't keep still, no use trying, I have cried Hurrah, hurrah, and our old gobbler has responded with a tiger every time. All alone, no one to talk to and ready to collapse, I was thankful for the turkey's attention. So, Mr. Editor, California can sit and weep that she cannot stay the tide of progress, and fifty years hence in history, won't the present Legislature and Governor of State appear to our people like long-eared horses?[1]

Now, shall there not be a State Jubilee, on the adoption of the Fifteenth Amendment, and would it not be a good idea to have a celebration in Sacramento City, and all turn out and show the Democracy of California, that we are alive and determined to live while they are nearly dead, and determined to die?[2] Would it not be a glorious thing, every town, village, city and mining camp in the State, send her new-made citizens with banners, transparencies and torches. The singers and musicians all combine to make a concert great as Camillo Urso's.[3] All our benevolent societies in fine regalia. Our military companies, masonic lodges, and *our* ELEVATOR have a chief's position in the Procession. Start our State Poem, Bro. Whitfield. Write our State Oration, Bro. Wm. Hall; and all you White Piners come over where you belong, and help to make this jubilee just what it should be—the grandest and best California has ever seen.[4] Let the mountains greet the plains, and San Francisco join hand with her sister cities. Let none plead poverty, every one exert themselves to show to the world around us, that great as the boon is, we appreciate it truly. Now, please, don't Mr. Editor, allow any one to think I expect to vote—I shall never do it, unless compelled to. I am so glad Mr. Trask can vote, and I will watch him, and woe to him if he should be caught voting the Democratic ticket. A Democrat told me a year ago he had no objections to Mr. Trask having the right of ballot, and said that was the universal expression in our city. I told him he did not wish to vote "by the leave of the Democracy, for he was pledged to eternal hatred towards so vile a thing as the Democracy of the Haight-stamp."[5] I think I had better stop for I cannot find a period in my feelings and will have to close at a comma.

—Semper Fidelis

1. California rejected the Fifteenth Amendment in late January of 1870 and did not ratify it until 1962. Georgia ratified the amendment on 2 February 1870; Iowa actually finished the ratification process the next day.
2. Bell and Carter's husband Dennis were both active in planning celebrations of the ratification of the Fifteenth Amendment.
3. One of the most noted violinists of the nineteenth century, Urso (1842–1902) toured the United States several times—often presenting massive concerts. She was scheduled to play in San Francisco later in February 1870, and both Carter and her readers probably saw publicity materials.
4. After writing *America and Other Poems* (1853), James Monroe Whitfield (1822–1871) moved to California c. 1861, where he worked as a barber in San Francisco, wrote regularly for the *Elevator*, and was active in California's black community; see Joan R. Sherman, *Invisible Poets: Afro-Americans in the Nineteenth Century*, 42–52. On Hall (c. 1823–?), see notes to Carter's letter published in the 7 August 1868 *Elevator*. The "White Piners" Carter refers to were blacks who had left the state for Nevada in search of silver; see Carter's 31 January 1869 letter in the 5 February 1869 *Elevator*. Both Whitfield and Hall, as well as the White Pine phenomena, are briefly discussed in Rusco, *Good Time Coming*.
5. Democrat governor of California Henry Haight.

Elevator 25 February 1870: 2

SAM OATES.
Mud Hill, Feb.20, '70.

Mr. Editor,—Our usually quiet city has been excited of late over an article that appeared in the Daily *Gazette*,[1] in which the editor compared the talent of the colored people of this place to that of the present Legislature of this State, and of course, the colored people took exception to it, not being willing to be classed with a traitorous set, and the editor of the *Gazette* was obliged to take back all he had said; and since, several articles have appeared in the paper giving Mr. Oates, Assemblyman from this place,[2] some hard hits; but not hard enough to penetrate his dull brain. This *Oates* is no more fit to be in the position he now disgraces, than a three year old calf. He is known here as a blatant Blacksmith, whose coarse unrefined manners never belonged to a gentlemen, and whose rough, political speeches have made him the laughing stock of the town; and the hate he evinced towards colored people has developed of late wonderfully, and he is now, to use his own words, "obliged to fight or emigrate," as he said he should, if the "Fifteenth Amendment become a law of the land." His talk of fighting is really laughable. When his country was in peril, he didn't do any fighting, and I will bet that he will emigrate twice before he will fight once.

Mr. Oates, it is well known, was once a Republican, and no doubt he thinks his Democratic brethren distrust him—so like the boy, who helped himself to bread, butter and sugar, he piles the sugar on so thick it won't stick; and I presume many of the members in Sacramento feel like taking hold of his huge shirt collar, and seating him when in the midst of his unreasonable speeches. Here, many recollect his political change; he ran on the Republican ticket and was defeated; the Post Office he sought was given to another,[3] and from that time he has sailed under Democratic colors. Now listen to his thundering eloquence in behalf of Democracy—Listen to his undying words: "Give me liberty or give me death." Oh! what a pity Patrick Henry should have uttered them first, from an original idea coming from *Samivel*,[4] would indeed be a wonder.

—Semper Fidelis

1. The *Nevada Daily Gazette*, a pro-Union and pro-Republican newspaper edited by Edwin F. Bean, the city's first Republican postmaster.

2. Sam T. Oates, a Cornish miner and blacksmith, was elected to the state assembly on an anti-Chinese, pro-white miner platform in 1869. His term there is discussed briefly in Ralph Mann, *After the Gold Rush: Society in Grass Valley and Nevada City, California 1849–1870*, 191.
3. California's patronage system was notorious—and regularly discussed in the newspapers of the day.
4. A play on both Oates's first name and ethnicity, this ironic reference to the character from Charles Dickens's *The Pickwick Papers* (Pickwick's servant, whose blend of sometimes-clichéd wisdom with a Cockney accent made him immensely popular with readers) questions Oates's racist version of populism.

⁓

Elevator 11 March 1870: 2
Mud Hill, March 5th, '70

Mr. Editor,—Hash is good to eat when one can get nothing else, and I propose to give you a mess, as I have a quantity on hand. Walking down the street today, I came up to a colored man, who was a hard looking object—ragged, filthy, and I should judge about half-drunk, as I was in the act of passing two men came up and passing him made this remark: "Fifteenth Amendment voter ain't it a—(with an oath). Shame, such things can vote." Now sir, look down the street if you please, there goes several men who look no better, than this specimen of humanity before you, and they are Anglo-Saxon, reared with every advantage of education, accustomed to good society from childhood, and they seek the low and debased, and you commonly find them where filth and drunkenness is, and they are voters, go to the polls reeling, and no one says, "aint it a shame such things can vote." Now this poor ignorant colored man has had no opportunity for elevation, born a slave and living such until fifty years old, his position only made endurable by deceit—his companions with himself have learned the vices of those over them, and who is responsible, and who will hold up clean hands? Not those two men who made that remark for the benefit of my ears, this morning; and I will tell them, for every drunken colored man who will go to the poll, I will say there will be ten drunken white men. I will tell these men, if they will reform their drunken and debased, I will go to work to effect the reformation of the colored man we met this morning.

Mr. Editor, please send me three copies of this number, for I wish those men to have each a copy.

In one of my articles lately,[1] I said I would not vote, unless compelled to, and I have received a letter asking me, "how such a thing can be possible," as there is no law compelling one to vote, I will suppose a case. In our city are two candidates for the Mayoralty, (we ain't had a Mayor yet) one is Republican, and the other a Democrat, and I think and believe one party is as strong as the other; one of my neighbors is a Democrat, and tells me she is going to vote, and hopes her candidate will be elected. My fears are aroused, and I cast my vote through a sense of duty to destroy the value of my neighbor's.

Our neighboring town has been doing honors to one of their departed dead, last week—and while all have tried to honor his memory, by words of praise, no one has had courage to remember his traitorous sentiments and influences during the great war. One of the friends of Sam Oates writes a note to me,[2] stating, that he Sam had always been a true friend to the colored man, always allowed them to drink in his saloon, (if they paid for it), and says Sam would drink with colored men too. I will say that was before Sam learned "that there was a law above Congress," and before that law had been written on his conscience by the finger of God—before he knew the "manhood of his race"—Oh, bosh, Sam, we expect to see you walk arm in arm with colored men soliciting their votes.

—Semper Fidelis

1. See Carter's 5 February 1870 letter in the 11 February 1870 *Elevator*.
2. See Carter's 20 February 1870 letter in the 25 February 1870 *Elevator*.

Elevator 15 April 1870: 3

Mr. Editor,—"It is hard to forget." These words I heard yesterday, and the question under discussion, was the character, politically, of a self announced candidate for the Marshal-ship of our little city; and the "hard to forget," was some ugly mean sayings of this candidate against colored men, when he thought they were not likely to get the right of franchise; and now being on the Republican ticket, of course all voters are desirable; and the man seems himself to have forgotten his bad words. Not so, however, the colored voters, and the "hard to forget," with such words as the following could be heard from many: "I'd rather vote for the Democratic nominee—I won't vote at all."

I say, let us stop and consider this question in all it bearings. What party has secured to us the great boon of freedom and franchise, not the Democratic. They could call us apes, monkeys, and a thousand other hard names, and shall we now prove ourselves apes and monkeys, by telling the world by our political course that we indorse [sic] their sayings as true. Again, we freely acknowledge that there are good and true men in the Democratic ranks, but they do not live up to their platform—which is *bad*. While we confess that many Republicans are bad and unsound, and we well know that the Republican platform is *sound and good*; but these do not fully endorse it. Many persons enter political parties, like teachers in schools, only half educated, and while instructing pupils are all the time learning, and after awhile find themselves educated up to the standard, as teachers by their position. So with many in the Republican ranks. Day by day are they growing into just views and righteous acts by the pressure of party—and because when they were young or just born into the party, they gave utterance to Democratic nasty sayings—shall we remember them in a way to strengthen the very party who taught them and still teaches that the black man is inferior and not worthy of his rights? No! Friends vote the Republican ticket out and out—the candidate has received an education among the Democrats, the platform will keep him straight, and your vote will help to educate him and sustain a party governed by justice and equality.

The example in the South, where by introducing conservative principles they sought to affiliate party, has wrought great misery. Let us profit by their example and not turn to the right or left, but vote the *black* Republican ticket, whether it be *long hair*, short hair or no hair at all.[1]

—Semper Fidelis

1. Carter takes a common slur used by Democrats—"black Republican"—and makes it racial rallying cry. The "long hair" and "short hair" voters were factions of the California Unionist Republican party. When Douglas Democrat-turned-Republican Senator John Conness (1821–1909) and his "short hairs" tried to place Governor Frederick F. Low (1828–1894) in the Senate seat held by hawkish Democrat John McDougall (1817–1867), the "long hairs," who supported George Gorham's faction of the party, objected. (For more on Gorham, see notes to Carter's letter of 6 September 1867 published in the 20 September 1867 *Elevator*.) After a violent meeting in Sacramento in July of 1865, Low withdrew from consideration, but the differences flared regularly throughout the rest of the 1860s and early 1870s.

Elevator 22 April 1870: 1

CELEBRATION IN NEVADA CITY.
Mud Hill, April 16, '70.

Mr. Editor,—The celebration here on the 12th was a decided success, and has done much to give influence to the colored people. Notwithstanding snow and mud in the morning, the Grass Valley folks were in time, and were met on the edge of the town by the Lincoln Club with music, and escorted to the Congregational Church, where all listened to a sermon by Rev. Alexander Packer, most appropriate to the occasion, and well received with approbation; for all know his war record here. He was one of Oberlin's students, who enlisted in the beginning of the strife—was a prisoner, and learned through suffering what *Liberty* is worth.[1] At the church a procession was formed, which was something to be proud of here in the *Sierras*, headed by *our* band, which can't be beat.[2] The school children, Lincoln Club, with their beautiful banner, citizens on foot and in carriages, marched through the principal streets, eliciting from many on the sidewalks, a hearty "God bless you," and "ain't this glorious," and even the Democrats wreathed their faces with smiles, and only one ventured to spit this spite. I don't know his name, or I would give it for the benefit of posterity—but I should know him by the shape of his nose. Mr. Editor, don't nature put a mark upon unreasonable people, so that they may be read at a glance?[3]

Pardon my digression. At the theatre, the procession entered, and there the exercises were most interesting; the best feature of the whole was the singing by the school children. Never was "America" warbled forth sweeter, than by the little ones. Mr. Ford, as President, made some very appropriate remarks—and what shall I say of the Oration by Rev. J.H. Hubbard?[4] I have been thinking of some word to express myself in regard to it, and can find only one that comprehends the whole thing that is "killing." I never saw an audience kept in such complete good nature, and never did the Democracy receive a more direct dressing. The past legislature was truthfully described, and I felt a spirit of thankfulness, that none of my kindred were in its desecrated halls. Mr. Cantine,[5] as Reader did well, and the Declaration of Sentiment was excellent. Great praise is due the Grass Valley people, who by purse and presence helped to make this a day long to be remembered in Nevada City; and to the friends who acted as Vice-Presidents, who by their money, helped this celebration along, our thanks are due. The day proved to be pleasant, the streets soon dried, and all walked about with ease until evening, when a grand ball wound up the affair here. In Grass Valley, Mr. Hubbard gave his oration in the evening, and I hope benefitted the Democracy of that place.

—Semper Fidelis.

1. Grass Valley is Nevada City's near neighbor. The Lincoln Club was one of Nevada City's black drill/social organizations. "Packer" was actually Alexander Parker (c. 1829–?), a Scottish immigrant who was one of several Oberlin College students—he was in the class of 1861 in the theology department—who joined Company C (the Oberlin Monroe Rifles) of the 7th Ohio Infantry. He was taken prisoner in August 1861, served time at the infamous Libby Prison, and was exchanged in May 1862. Discharged in July 1863, he moved to California, where he preached in Los Angeles in 1860s and farmed in Siskiyou County—though he remained active in the Scottish Congregational Church. See Lawrence Wilson, *Itinerary of the 7th Ohio Volunteer Infantry*; Theodore Wilder, *History of Company C of the 7th Regiment of Ohio Volunteer Infantry*, and 1870 Census of Siskiyou County, California, 626.
2. The band was lead by Carter's husband.
3. Carter refers to the popular pseudo-science of physiognomy.
4. Nathaniel Ford (c. 1827–?) was a barber in Nevada City; see 1870 Census of Nevada County, California, 278, and 1860 Census of Sierra County, California, 881. James H. Hubbard (22 July 1838–after 1887), a Baltimore-born free black man, attended the Allegheny Institute in Pennsylvania for two years before moving to California. He was converted at a Methodist revival in Nevada City in 1855, married (to Josephine Carson), and licensed to preach. His first charge, in 1861, was Grass Valley. A protégé of Thomas M. D. Ward, he was active in forming the California Conference, and, by 1869, was an elder. He later served in the Missouri and Colorado Conferences. See "Rev. J. H. Hubbard of the Colorado Conference," *Christian Recorder*, 14 July 1887.
5. George A. Cantine (c. 1823–?), a New York-born laborer who lived on Church Street in Nevada City; see 1880 Census of Nevada County, 22D.

Elevator 8 July 1870: 3
Mud Hill, June 29th, 1870

Mr. Editor,—"Semper Fidelis, why don't you write for the ELEVATOR?" Such is the query coming to me from friends, and I will say to them, 'tis not that I do not love the ELEVATOR as well as ever, but I love rest more, for I am afflicted with rheumatism, and find writing more painful than anything else I do.[1] I made a promise many years ago to write True Montague's Autobiography,[2] and whenever I can I am laboring to fulfil[l] that promise, for well I know that the years that spare none are hurrying me on, and the great "Reaper Death," is laying low those who could assist True to make her history more correct than it could otherwise be; and I feel anxious to avail myself of all the dates and facts by her forgotten, so I have written many letters, and my harvest gathered from them may some day fill a space in the ELEVATOR. Until I have the matter arranged, I yield all my space in the paper to the Professor for the advocacy of "Woman's Rights," having this week met Mrs. Pitt-Stevens, the Editor of the *Pioneer*, who tells me Brother G____d is a co-worker.[3]

—Semper Fidelis.

1. Carter's silence in the months previous to the publication of this piece did occasion comment. Bell wrote in the 24 June 1870 *Elevator* that "We miss the contributions of this talented lady. Want of time has prevented us from writing to her ere this, but at the urgent request of several friends and correspondents, we solicit a continuance of her literary favors. Bro. G____d is very earnest in his desire to see her again in print." ("Bro. G____d" may be J. E. M. Gilliard, a sometime-contributor to the *Elevator*.) Further, in the 8 July 1870 issue, Bell published a letter from F. H. Grice of Elko, Nevada, that said, in part, "Mr. Editor, it has been over three months since I saw the name of your learned lady correspondent, 'Semper Fidelis' in the columns of the ELEVATOR. Has she deserted us? Is her ardor for our intellectual and moral advancement less sanguine since the ratification of the Fifteenth Amendment? I sincerely hope that her name ere long will be in the columns of the ELEVATOR with her interesting articles, and to let our people on the Pacific Coast know that 'Semper Fidelis' is still among the living, and still faithful, and in full intellectual vigor." Grice (c. 1837–?) was an early daguerreotypist who lived for some years in California before moving to Elko, where he worked as a hotel porter. Then, seemingly because he had Mormon ties, he moved to Salt Lake City, Utah; some sources suggest his family eventually suffered discrimination in Utah and later moved to Idaho. (See 1870 Census of Elko County, Nevada, 37, and 1880 Census of Salt Lake County, Utah, 288A.) The publication of Carter's 8 July 1870 piece led Bell to note that "We welcome this lady again to our columns. Without our ever faithful correspondent, the ELEVATOR would lose one of its distinguished features."
2. See Carter's letters of 29 May 1869 in the 4 June 1869 *Elevator* and 14 August 1869 in the 20 August 1869 *Elevator*.
3. Emily Pitts (1844–?), who took over the *Sunday Evening Mercury*, turned it into the *Pioneer* in 1869, and was at the forefront of the California Women's Suffrage Association. Her marriage to railroad secretary Augustus A. Stevens did little to slow her fights for women's rights (the *Pioneer* was typeset by women) and temperance. See Rebecca J. Mead, *How the Vote Was Won: Women's Suffrage in the Western U.S., 1868–1914*.

Elevator 18 May 1872: 2
Mud Hill, May 6, 1872

Mr. Editor,—When will man know himself? I fear never—and my mind has been awakened of late in regard to this matter, and much have I thought of the political fizzle at Cincinnati, and the part taken by Horace Greeley.[1] It is a well known fact that many of our men in old age undo the work of a life-time, and among our public men it is a noticeable fact. The first sermon I recollect in my life was preached by a Baptist minister who had seceded from the Scotch Presbyterians.[2] He was in the vigor of manhood, and his effort was pronounced wonderful, and my child ears heard every argument and treasured them up in memory, and when I was thirty years of age I heard him again, and still preaching as a Baptist, he gave a strong Presbyterian doctrinal sermon. Bowen will probably win.[3] Josiah T. Walls,[4] who represents the State of Florida, was born at Winchester, Virginia in 1842; received a common school education, and claims to be a planter. He is slight in stature, of rather light complexion, close, curly hair, dresses well, and wears gay neckties. He has not been in his seat since the early days of the session. The only thing known from him is a long speech, which he reads with the manner of a rustic sc[h]oolmaster.

Benjamin Stirling Turner,[5] of Alabama, is a large, broad shouldered man, with a very large, flat nose, curly hair, and, in physique, at least, intensely suggestive undoing his former effort; and when I told him what he had done, he said to me he always preached so and the change must be in me. So Mr. Greeley. After a consistent political life down to the close of the war, and after molding the minds of thousands, helping to educate our nation into great principles of justice and right, working with an energy unequaled, has at last succumbed to the selfish part of his nature and stands before the world undoing his life work, having just been won from right by his sympathy for Jeff Davis in hoops.[6] Our Seward has shown the same weakness, and his "irrepressible conflict," after being carried on by him for years with vigor, power and great results, he found at last it conflicted with his advanced age, and was repressible, and he has shown to the world the falsity of that proverb, "old men for counsel and young men for war."[7] Much beloved Wendell Phillips is drifting in the same channel, and our dear Sumner is surely weakening.[8] Is it to be wondered at when we realize the mental struggle these men have endured, the more than martyrdom they have passed through; for years they went ahead of public opinion, sneered at by nearly the whole nation—they have lived to see their opinions popular, but so used to the strife have they become that they cannot let their weary and worn minds rest, but seek to undo what they have done, but going back; but all the while believing they are going forward. At just what age men's usefulness ceases, I know not, but I do think my day of usefulness has passed, and, for fear I may undo what I have done, I write very little.

—Semper Fidelis

P.S.—A mistake in my last, [it was] "I who cut the cake," not Bro Sanks[9] as it reads in the ELEVATOR.

—S.F.

1. Best known as a newspaperman, Greeley (1811–1872) was nominated for President by the Liberal Republicans, a breakaway faction of the Republican party who felt that Reconstruction was essentially complete and saw the Grant administration as hopelessly corrupt and ineffective. Because this sense was shared by Democrats, Greeley was also nominated at their convention. On Greeley, see Robert C. Williams, *Horace Greeley: Champion of American Freedom*.

2. This combination of Baptist and Scotch Presbyterian sentiment sounds similar to the version of Cambellite Christianity that may have been practiced by Carter's mysterious first husband; see the introduction to this volume.

3. Probably Christopher Columbus Bowen (1832–1880), a Confederate veteran and Charleston, South Carolina, lawyer who served as a Republican member of Congress from 1868 to 1871; he lost the election Carter refers to. See Albert Mackey, *The Political Treason of Senator F. A. Sawyer and Representative C. C. Bowen*.

4. A Virginia-born slave who was forced into the Confederate Army, captured, and allowed to join the U.S. Colored Troops, Walls (1842–1905) settled in Florida and was twice sent to Congress—and twice unseated after his opponents contested his victories. See Peter D. Klingman, *Josiah Walls*.

5. A slave born in North Carolina, Sterling (1825–1894) was a Republican member of Congress from Alabama from 1871 to 1873 and a delegate to the Republican National Convention in 1880. See *Black Americans in Congress, 1870–1989*.

6. Greeley had always challenged the South in his New York *Tribune* and was well known in antislavery and reform circles, but he stunned many when he put up bond for former Confederate President Jefferson Davis in 1867.

7. William Henry Seward (1801–1872), a Whig and then Republican who served in the U.S. Senate and then the Lincoln and Johnson cabinets as secretary of state, withdrew himself from active involvement in the civil rights struggles in the 1870s; see John M. Taylor, *William Henry Seward*. Generally ascribed to Cicero, the quoted proverb also appears in Frances Ellen Watkins Harper's 1892 novel *Iola Leroy*.

8. Phillips (1811–1884), arguably the antislavery movement's greatest white orator, had shifted his efforts to Native American issues, women's rights, and temperance—especially after it was clear that the Fifteenth Amendment would become reality. See James Brewer Stewart, *Wendell Phillips: Liberty's Hero*. Sumner (1811–1874) had been both an antislavery stalwart and an early champion of Reconstruction-era civil rights efforts for African Americans. Tension grew quickly between President Grant and Sumner, though, and the disillusioned

Sumner joined with Greeley and the Liberal Republicans in the election of 1872. See David
Herbert Donald, *Charles Sumner*.

9. The issue of the *Elevator* to which Carter refers is missing. Born a slave in North
Carolina, Isaac Sanks (c. 1814–?) bought and freed his wife Chasey (c. 1831–?) with money
made as a pilot on the Florida coast. She then bought him. The two became important
members of Grass Valley's black community; Sanks worked as a miner, Wells Fargo janitor,
laborer, and ice cream parlor owner. He was active in the fights for black male suffrage and
equal educational opportunity. See Pat Jones, "Nevada County's Black Pioneers," as well as
the 1860 Census of Nevada County, California, 236; the 1870 Census of Nevada County,
California, 325, and the 1880 Census of Nevada County, California, 78A.

⌒

Elevator 18 January 1873: 2

EMANCIPATION CELEBRATION IN MARYSVILLE, ETC.
Marysville, January 7th 1863 [sic]:

Mr. Editor:—

"Still achieving,
Still pursuing,
Learn to labor and to wait,"[1]

And then reap results; and how great the harvest may become has just
been realized in this city. There is no use in my telling you why Marysville
had a celebration on the 1st, but that she did have one and that one the
greatest one ever held on the Pacific coast, I can assure you.[2] The weather was
unpropitious, rain and mud rendering it impossible to make as fine a procession as desirable and as was anticipated, and yet there was no failure—no,
far [from] it. I don't know who put it into the heads of the Sherman Guard
of this city to receive the Sacramento Zouaves with military honors, but that
they did it, in the face of all previous examples, it worthy of note, and to
Capt. Newhart and his company belong the honor of being the first in the
car of progress to do away with prejudice[3]; and the city of Marysville belongs
the honor of making the initiatory movement to do away with caste. Oh,
how great our job to witness this great progressive movement for the right,
and to learn that no one had been injured by the contact.

At 12 [P.] M. of the first arrived the Sacramento Zouaves, accompanied by many friends making a delegation of two hundred. As they were escorted by the Sherman Guard through the prinicipal streets, and with the firing of cannons, ringing of bells, and music of two bands, it made us forget the bad weather, and we said "we have labored and waited long for this and now we know the world moves,"[4] and we sighed as we saw both companies march in the armory to stack arms; we wished it were possible for both companies to march side by side through every town of our Golden State, and show to the people that at least the black man is capable of becoming a thorough drilled soldier, and so proficient that he may teach the white man. I viewed with more than ordinary interest the precision of drill by the company of Zouaves, and my mind went back to 1858 when Colonel Ellsworth drilled his celebrated company[5] in a public square fronting my door, and for three months every day, rain or shine, they would be seen going through the tactics that made his company so celebrated in all the principal cities of the United States which they visited and which at least gained him an early death and a hero's crown. I often think how little any of us can foresee events even if shadows are cast before. In the same city where Colonel Ellsworth drilled his celebrated company he became the affianced of a young lady, the daughter of a banker who would not give his consent to the marriage of his daughter until Colonel Ellsworth had some profession aside from arms. He procured for him a position at Springfield, Illinois, to revise the military code of the State and there, when he had that completed he went into the law office of the immortal Lincoln, soon to leave it for, the profession of arms which his country so much needed. I do not think his company surpassed the Sacramento Zouaves on parade.

Oh how much one may lose by being a woman. I learned at Marysville; for after the Zouaves and Sherman Guard stacked arms, then lunch came in order, and a bounteous one had been prepared by the Grant & Wilson Club of Marysville,[6] from which women were excluded, and that portion of the celebration, with its toasts and speeches I lost. Some of it I got second-handed, and the best I heard was that Dr. Wilkins (who, you recollect, was sent by Governor Haight to Europe to inspect insane asylums) and he was converted.[7] Now we will all pray he may not backslide but even work for equal rights to all, regardless of color or previous condition.

The theater was filled to listen to the exercises of the day, and the opening address by Mr. Duplex, President of the day was commended for good sense and brevity, and the reading of the Emancipation Proclamation by Miss Powers was well received, and I should be glad to see her in the High School at Marysville, where she belongs.[8] The oration, by Mr. Small, was, of course full of telling points, yet, not delivered with his usual force, owing to a throat affection I believe.[9] It was received with applause and pronounced just right by all but Irishmen, which will appear to you upon reading, very apparent. The poem, by Mr. Jenkins,[10] was pronounced good, and thus ended the exercises of the day, all being conducted with the utmost decorum. After a short rest all went back to the theater to witness the wonderful tap drill of the Zouaves. Mr. Badger, one of Marysville's large hearted citizens,[11] entered with full spirit into the arrangement for the evening's entertainment, and arranged a programme which gave a great amount of pleasure to as crowded a house as I ever entered. The tap-drill was the gem of the whole performance, however; while the singing of the Sacramento Glee Club[12] was good, the solo singer possessed a very sweet voice which she handled as well as did the conductor his baton. Much to the amusement of the audience Professor Bowlin[13] gave as exquisite performance on the violin. The evening's entertainment closed with two tableaux, War and Freedom.[14] They were grand indeed.

It would seem by this time all were weary enough to rest but to very many the best was to come, and all haste was made to prepare for the ball. And, Mr. Editor, you were needed to describe beauty and dress, for both were present, and I, as a lookeron, cannot tell who was the belle of the room, for all looked like belles to me and really the taste displayed was most pleasing; and I was told by residents of the city no party was ever given where better dressing or dancing could be seen. My friend B. Cogar disputed the beauship with Heuston [sic] Saunders, both gentlemen looking charming.[15] The most noticeable feature was the absence of caste; and glad was I that the citizens of Marysville participated so largely in the enjoyment of the evening. I was told repeatedly we are all alike now, caste has fled; but, in a few days I learned it had found a resting-place in the cemetery, where by mistake, a colored woman was buried in the part allotted to white people, and she was to be disenterred. Her husband informed me he had a deed for the lot, and yet he was told he must consent to her removal or have trouble.[16] I wonder if some people will not attempt to drive the black man from heaven. Now friend Bell, you missed much in not being at the celebration. Your friends regretted your absence, and I would [have] liked you to have seen what was really an ovation to the Zouaves. I saw your Most Worshipful Grand Master, Peter Anderson present, mingling with the guests—and of course he could report for the *Appeal*.[17] More next week.

—Semper Fidelis.

1. The concluding lines of "A Psalm of Life," by Henry Wadsworth Longfellow (1807–1882).
2. Carter's readers would have known that this was an Emancipation Day celebration.
3. Well known among California's black community, the Sacramento Zouaves were one of the premier black drill companies. D. D. Carter attended at least one of their famous Emancipation performances in Sacramento on 1 January 1872; see 29 December 1871 *Elevator*. "Capt. Newhart" was probably the Ohio-born James Newhart (c. 1843–?) who owned a Marysville saloon. See 1870 Census of Yuba County, California, 609, and 1880 Census of Butte County, California, 240C.
4. This quote seems to allude to the piece's epigraph from Longfellow.
5. Elmer E. Ellsworth (1837–1861) was a key early advocate of zouave-style drill. He met Lincoln in December of 1859, when his Zouave Company toured twenty cities; it seems likely that Carter alludes to this tour, too. After briefly working in his law office, Ellsworth enlisted. He was shot when removing a Confederate flag from the rooftop of an Alexandria, Virginia hotel. The "young lady" referred to later in the paragraph was Carrie Spofford. See Ruth Painter Randall, *Colonel Elmer Ellsworth*.
6. A Republican club; the Wilson named here was Grant's running mate Henry Wilson (1812–1875).
7. Edmund T. Wilkins (1824–1891), a doctor and plantation owner who brought thirteen slaves with him to California and freed them in 1854. He toured asylums in Europe in 1870 and early 1871 before becoming active in state reforms to the treatment of the mentally ill. See Howard A. Kelly, *Dictionary of American Medical Biography*.
8. Probably Martha Jane Powers (1857–1889), the daughter of Peter Powers and Rachel Seals. The elder Powers was born into slavery in Missouri in 1828, lived in Marysville in the 1860s, and moved to Chico in 1870; he was active as a teacher while in both Marysville and Chico. Martha Jane married Alfred Jefferson Logan. See Beasley, *Negro Trail Blazers*.
9. On Small, see Carter's 8 January 1869 letter in the 15 January 1869 *Elevator*.
10. I have not yet identified which "Mr. Jenkins" this is; he may be the J. L. Jenkins listed in the 1870 Yuba County, California census, 634, with the Edward Duplex family.
11. I have not yet identified "Mr. Badger."
12. One of a number of African American musical and social clubs.
13. I have not yet identified "Professor Bowlin."
14. Tableaux vivants were common in the late nineteenth century.
15. Benjamin Cogar (c. 1835–?), an Illinois-born barber who settled in Sacramento, and Huston Saunders (c. 1843–?), a Delaware-born barber who also settled in Sacramento; see 1870 Census of Sacramento County, California, 241 and 347.
16. Racial segregation of cemeteries lasted well into the twentieth century.
17. Anderson (c. 1822–1879) was, as per the introduction to this volume and notes above, Bell's chief journalistic rival.

Elevator 25 January 1873: 2
Mud Hill, January 17, 1873

Mr. Editor:—Judge of my great surprise on receiving the last Elevator and to see no report of the celebration in Marysville in its columns.[1] I am sure my letter will read strange to many. I supposed you had received a full report, and I was to pick up crumbs and that is just what I am doing now.

A friend in Marysville told me he was opposed to a first of January celebration, believing we ought to let all recollection of former years die out. I have thought much of his words since, and I must say I think them altogether wrong. It is an established fact that our appreciation of everything is commensurate with its cost, and our fathers well understood that fact, and so gathered every item of the great struggle that gave America her independence, gave it to us in history; for our schools in paintings for our parlors, and monuments for our public squares, and still fearing or forgetful they even keep the great anniversary day—July 4th. And decreed it should be celebrated by American citizens to all coming time. Now have we not more to remember than they? What was the oppression of the British yoke compared to slavery, taxation to stripes? Was there ever anything so unhuman, so devilan as American slavery? Could the graves of its victims open and their dead come forth—think you they would say "cease to remember," no! their words would be "cry aloud to your children, and let childrens' children never forget what liberty cost, never forget Emancipation Day; never forget the immortal Lincoln, who by God's permission gave us that great day, which has brought together many long seperated families, husbands and wives, parents and children which cruel slavery had seperated.["] I think every American ought on that day to rejoice, let them be colored or white, and all ought, as in Marysville, unite in celebrating the Emancipation Act; and, also, as orderly citizens in a becoming manner, avoid of drunkedness, for not one drunken person did I see on that day. And none should fear getting too much piety in such gatherings, for God has said, "Righteousness exalts a nation; but sin is a reproach to any people."[2]

When I looked around the theatre in Marysville and saw colored and white sitting together in every part of the house, I thought of my text, especially the latter clause of it: "Learn to labor and to wait."[3] Three years ago I went to the same theatre, accompanied by a lady whose skin was dark enough to class her as colored, and they wanted her to go in the gallery,[4] I told them then what I thought, and said "not much longer will we have to wait;" and thank God the waiting is done. Right here by me sits one who went to Marysville to attend an agricultural fair about the year 1860; and Wednesday morning he went to the gate and was refused admittance. They told him on Friday, he could go in,—that day being set apart for colored folks. He has it in his heart against Marysville to this day, and when I tell how nobly the citizens did this first of January he said "They had better do works meet for repentance."

I accompanied Mrs. Duplex to the colored school.[5] It is taught in the basement of the Baptist Church and is small in numbers, only thirteen children were in attendance. I found the room furnished with modern furniture, maps, and a faithful teacher, who has had charge of the school only one week. I was convinced no discipline had been maintained by the previous teacher, and I earnestly implore the parents to give the teacher their cooperation and see that their children do obey, for I can assure them they will lift great burdens from the teacher's shoulders, and reap a harvest of joy in the conduct of their children. Again, parents should see that their children are in school every day, for nothing serves more to discourage a child than to have his class ahead of him; and by all means the child should be encouraged to steady attendance. Parents, visit the school often, and see for yourselves the progress your children are making.

While in Marysville I stopped with your friends, Mr. and Mrs. McGowan,[6] and to him and his family I am under obligations for hospitality extended, and that I dearly love Marysville with its long streets, wide side walks, and beautiful gardens I can assure you; and that I love the dear friends there better than all is truth; and the great celebration there will be a joy to me forever; for in it I see the fulfillment of learning to "labor and to wait."

—Semper Fidelis

(We regret not having received any notice of the celebration except that furnished by "Semper Fidelis," last week. We did expect to have received a copy of the oration and the poem, or at all events a synopsis of the proceedings. Mr. Duplex wrote that he had sent us a paper containing a report of the proceedings, which we have not received.—Ed. El.[7])

1. See Carter's "Emancipation Celebration in Marysville" in the 18 January 1873 *Elevator*.
2. Proverbs 14:34. See Kachun, *Festivals of Freedom*, for a discussion of Carter's assertion here.
3. The final lines from Longfellow's "A Psalm of Life."
4. This passage suggests that Carter's skin was fairly light—light enough to allow her to avoid the gallery.

5. Edward Duplex's wife is (or wives are) listed as Elizabeth (c. 1837 in Virginia–?) and Sophia (c. 1838 in New York–?) in the 1870 Census of Yuba County, California, 634, and the 1880 Census of Yuba County, California, 450C, respectively. On this family, see Carter's letter of 8 January 1869 in the 15 January 1869 *Elevator* and her "Emancipation Celebration in Marysville" in the 18 January 1873 *Elevator*.

6. Jesse McGowan (c. 1816–?), an Ohio-born barber who sometimes spelled his name "MacGowan," and Dorothy (c. 1830–?), a Virginia-born laundress, who owned significant real estate in Marysville. See Lapp, *Blacks in Gold Rush California*, as well as the 1870 Census of Yuba County, California, 577, and the 1880 Census of Yuba County, California, 397A.

7. Duplex did sometimes contribute to the *Elevator*.

⌒

Elevator 1 February 1873: 2

FROM OUR UP-COUNTRY CORRESPONDENT.
Mud Hill, January 24th, 1873

Mr. Editor:—Many years ago, when visiting Dussledorff Gallery in New York I saw a painting entitled: "Waiting for the verdict,"[1] and while looking at it I saw a world of meaning, and I saw depicted on that canvass the varied passions of hope and fear so vividly portrayed, that to me the faces were agonized, and I turned away weeping. A friend who was with me said, 'tis only a picture. Since then I have seen the reality, and have witnessed upturned faces, heaving chests, sunken eyes, hollow cheeks, and never have I felt deeper grief than when looking at that masterpiece. Now, for four days I have been here waiting to give in my testimony, and by me has been an anxious wife whose husband is arranged at the bar for a criminal offense; and while waiting to go upon the stand to testify, I have tried to imagine myself "waiting for a verdict" when a loved one was on trial, and I can only think God help her.[2] And, Mr. Editor, I have had other reflections too, for I find a great unwillingness in people to testify even when they know anything about a case.

I cannot blame them when every effort is made to confuse witnesses, and when vulgarity is the rule, not the exception. I have seen timid women so questioned that they knew not what they were saying, and yet they were truthful, and their testimony would convict if guilty and exonerate the innocent. And oh! my heart has ached to think all respect has fled from our halls of justice, and our courts are filled with shysters who spout and blow and who do not respect either age or sex. With me, 'tis a matter of conscience, for I have found myself in places and in circumstances I had no idea could ever occur, and I know not how soon again I may find myself in extremity, and so I will by the help of God always be ready to speak the truth in behalf of those who are in extremity. I think if a few noble determined intelligent ladies would fearless[ly] take a stand and frown down all foolish questioning in a short time trials would cease to be farces and real criminals would tremble and the innocent would fear nothing. If men do not do better soon, I shall be in favor of women taking judicial positions, for I know that they could not do worse than men are doing now; so, Mr. Editor, if things do not change, I shall have to help the women roll the car along; and if, ever I get upon me the judicial robe, I will make the lawyers tremble.[3] So all shysters may take care.

—Semper Fidelis

1. A genre scene filled with suspense and depicting a family just outside of a British courtroom, this painting by Abraham Solomon (1803–1862) was widely shown, as were copies of the work. The original is now owned by the Tate Gallery. The Dussledorff was founded in 1849 and featured American and European (especially German) genre painting; Hiram Powers's famous statue *The Slave* was also exhibited there in the late 1850s.
2. I have not yet identified the incidents described here. The fight to make black testimony admissible in California was both long and hard; see Lapp, *Afro-Americans in California*, and Daniels, *Pioneer Urbanites*, for more information.
3. Carter's comments here—however humorously designed—offer an interesting counterpoint to her stance on women's suffrage.

***

Elevator 1 March 1873: 3

FROM OUR UP-COUNTRY CORRESPONDENT.
Mud Hill, Feb. 23d, 1873

Mr. Editor:—On one of the prominent hills of your city stands a building dedicated to knowledge. It is a grand and imposing structure several stories in height; the grounds surrounding it are laid out with taste, ornamented with flowers always in bloom; and wandering among them with books in hand young ladies and gentlemen, gathering from the beautiful, surroundings fresh inspirations for study. Within the building my vision is greeted with all the appliances of this day and age to make the pursuit of knowledge easy; in a chair I see seated a professor of languages, with a class of students before him translating Greek and Latin into English, Homer and Virgil becoming almost as familiar to those pupils as Bryant and Longfellow to us. I leave that room and enter another and there I see a class of young ladies reading French while before them is seated the madam, who can give them the proper accent with all the gesture which make a distinguishing feature of a Frenchman. After listening a while and becoming satisfied that they will be able to speak French in France, I pass into another department and see a philosophical apparatus; before me are boys and girls preparing themselves for the pursuits of life, some to fill the position of teachers, others as chemists in laboratories of their own to perfect discoveries which will bless future ages and make them immortal. Among them are many, who by inventive genius and cultivated minds will be able to revolutionize machinery and perchance invent perpetual motion. I stayed long enough among them to know that they surpass me in knowledge, and I went up to the observatory, where a complete astronomical apparatus is before me; a large telescope, well and firmly mounted where in pleasant nights can be studied the geography of the heavens and a comet seeker, by which those restless wanderers through space can be seen in time to give us notes of warning of their approach and collision with our earth. There I see a few, who night after night, with a love for science scan the heavens, all the time feeling like the psalmist of old. "When I consider the heavens, the work of thy hands, what is man that thou visiteth him?"[1] By and by they have their reward. A new planet is world born and the memory of them cannot die while the stars live and shine. I feel my littleness and want of knowledge, and thank God others have such opportunities. When the bell rings for prayers I enter the assembly; I listen to music led by Prof. Trask, and oh! the beautiful singing—nothing like it on the Pacific coast; and I thought 'tis like heaven and then I asked when was this grand institute born—what called it into being. I was answered "It was when war moved the hearts of men—when a Starr King lived and by his matchless eloquence moved the hearts of men of Anglo-Saxon birth and strained the hearts of the parents of these young ladies and gentlemen of color to desire great things for their children, and let them cope with others in the race of life."[2] Then the Livingstone Institute was born, and here it is.[3] Oh! Mr. Editor, it was a dream.

—Semper Fidelis

1. Drawn from Psalm 8:3–4, which reads "When I consider thy heavens, the work of thy
   fingers, the moon and the stars, which thou hast ordained; what is man, that thou art
   mindful of him? and the son of man, that thou visitest him?"
2. Thomas Starr King; see notes to Carter's letter of 4 July 1868 published in the 10 July 1868
   Elevator.
3. The Livingstone Institute was planned to be a secondary school for African Americans
   in the West (at times, plans suggested collegiate aspirations, too). Planning and fund-
   raising were interrupted by the Civil War and repeated charges of mismanagement. Black
   newspapers and black Californians generally were still debating the idea's demise well into
   the early 1870s, and the *Elevator* ran occasional pieces questioning where the funds raised
   had gone. For discussion of the Institute plans in the mid-1870s, see, for example, the
   14 September 1872 and 11 January 1873 issues of the *Pacific Appeal*.

~

Elevator 17 May 1873: 3
Mud Hill, May 5th, 1873

Mr. Editor:—The pleasure I enjoyed in glancing at Mr. Still's book[1] has awakened many incidents in my mind of escapes from slavery in another road
not named in his book, and which if written out would make a volume of
thrilling horror, and with now and then a note of joy. Oh! how often have
I wished some one competent would write out the history of the "Underground Railroad," from the Mississippi River to Chicago; for hundreds of
slaves escaped from Missouri, and if not retaken before reaching Chicago,
they found an asylum in Canada. In the year 1848 I was living in Wisconsin
near the Illinois line, and thought myself far from the Railroad, and for
many months I had not seen a fugitive or did not dream of my house being
known to any wishing to escape. It was a warm sunny day in June and I sat
rocking my little son in my arms; I fell into a daze, and that I was asleep I
know, for some one touched me lightly on my cheek and I went to singing
half awake, thinking my baby had awaked.[2] I opened my eyes and oh! what
a sight before me. A woman with scarcely clothing to cover herself and a
baby not three months old, and both nearly famished. She told me to hide
her quick for her master was in town, for she had seen him pass when laying in an old shed where she had been from midnight. Six long weeks she
had been on her way from Canton, Mo.,[3] traveling only by night and all the
time in fear of pursuit, living as best she could by milking cows; hungry and
nearly naked, with feet bleeding she came to me. I asked her why she came,

she told me she saw me when I was in Canton in March, and heard me say that I came down the river, and that Galena was on Fever River, which emptied in the Mississippi, and twelve miles from that I lived;[4] so she had traveled to find me, and the last night before reaching our place, had stayed in a barn in Galena, when she overheard two men talking about a reward of three hundred dollars for an escaped slave and child; one said to the other I wish I could get the money. She told me she squeezed her baby's mouth, for fear it would cry.

What to do, I did not know; yet I believed the Lord had led her to me, for she had stopped only across the alley from my house, and when I opened the door and sat down to hush my baby to sleep, she saw and knew me. For three days she spent her time in my cellar, and when bedtime she could rest. Then I took my buggy and rode out of town, just at evening and when it was dark, she came to me and I drove twenty-eight miles to a Quaker family, and at two o'clock I roused them up and left Dextra Hogan[5] with those who would care for her as she cared for her baby; for to save it from the trader she endured everything but death. I drove back within ten miles of home and visited a friend where I remained until near night; when I arrived at home I was asked: where baby and I had been; I told them to visit Mrs. H_____; and none to this day knew what a ride I took that night with my baby in my arms and the mother love in my heart going out towards that homeless mother and baby.

—Semper Fidelis

P.S. I think Dextra was mistaken about seeing her master in our place, as I heard he went no further than Galena.

1. The seminal *The Underground Rail Road* (Philadelphia: Porter and Coates, 1872) by Philadelphia activist William Still (1821–1902) was widely advertised in *The Elevator*, in part because Philip Bell was the book's West Coast agent. (Indeed, in addition to ads, Bell published excerpts in his paper.) See Larry Gara, "William Still," and, more generally, Gara's *The Liberty Line.*

2. This is the only reference Carter makes to having a child, and it seems to be contradicted by her obituary.

3. Canton is in northeast Missouri, not far from the Illinois border.

4. This would put Carter's home somewhere near Hazel Green, Wisconsin.

5. I have not yet identified "Dextra Hogan."

Elevator 19 July 1873: 2
Mud Hill, July 12th, 1873

Mr. Editor,—I have failed to keep my word on account of illness. I am glad, however, at this time to resume my pen and furnish for the ELEVA-TOR another sketch of the dark days before the war.[1] In the year 1851, early one morning I was called to the door to see a stranger, who told my girl that he had a message for me, and on going I saw a large portly black man, who delivered to me a note from the President of the anti-slavery society of Chicago[2] asking me to "assist the bearer by all means within my power." I asked him in and learned his history. An escape from slavery he repeated, which thrilled my nerves, and which I doubt that for hair breadth escapes from blood hounds and their equally blood-thirsty masters has no parallel in history. Now he was free. Through the aid of friends his freedom had been purchased (after his master was certain he could not capture him) for the sum of $1,800, and his wife and five children were in bondage, and he was going from place to place telling his life story and soliciting aid to make up an amount of over five thousand dollars to purchase his wife and children; and the *humane* master wrote—that only three months would be given to him to redeem them, if not paid by that time, he "would sell them to the trader," and the letter which I read had this gentlemanly expression. "Tell the _____ abolitionist[s] to go to hell and get the money for you. C. Young." The place was small where I lived, and I could only get the schoolhouse for the lecture. I went all around, asked every one to come and hear the man tell the story of his wrongs; and when evening came, a full house was present, and in fact, all around the house were men standing, and by each window there was a dozen heads.

The man told his story, but to my nervous, anxious brain, I thought without half the earnestness needed, or in language not half as forcible as he had told it to me in the morning. One after another of the heads at the window disappeared, and I was so disappointed. When he was done and a collection was taken there was only nine dollars. I counted the money, and was going to make some remarks in his behalf, when he asked me to wait until after he had sung an appropriate song. Oh, what a voice, and what a song. I suppose most of the readers of the ELEVATOR have heard it. And I will only give one verse:

I heard that Queen Victoria said,
    If we would all forsake,

Our native land of slavery,
    And come across the lake—
She was standing on the shore
    With arms extended wide,
To give us all a peaceful home
    Beyond the rolling tide.
CHORUS.
        —Old master don't come after me,
            I'm on my way to Canada,
    Where colored men are free.[3]

I looked around, the windows were full once more; the people were weeping and when he sat down, from every part of the house could be heard the dropping of money into hats, and from outdoors came the cry: "come and get our money"; and those English miners in the lead mines loved their Queen better than ever,[4] and said as they drop'd their money: "in the name of our gracious Victoria I give this"; and when I counted the money there was one hundred and ninety-six dollars. I did not get a chance to make my speech. I only said I thank you. They called for the song again, and I believe they would have staid all night if he had continued to sing. The next day I went to visit some of the rich men of our place, and two of them each gave me fifty dollars for him, and while his words failed to reach the hearts of the multitude his song did most effectually.

—Semper Fidelis[5]

1. None of Carter's work appeared in the *Elevator* between her 5 May 1873 letter (in the 17 May 1873 *Elevator*) and this letter.
2. Chicago's Anti-Slavery Society was formed in 1840, but by the late 1840s, a variety of other antislavery groups—including a vigilance association, a women's group, and various informal black groups—were also active. See Glennette Tilley Turner, *The Underground Railroad in Illinois*.
3. Generally attributed to abolitionist songster George Washington Clark (c. 1812–?) under the title "The Free Slave," this song was quite popular among antislavery activists by the late 1840s; see Daniel G. Hill, *The Freedom Seekers: Blacks in Early Canada*. Indeed, variations of it appear in Martin Delany's novel *Blake* (1859), Sarah Bradford's *Scenes in the Life of Harriet Tubman* (1869), and J. D. Green's 1864 slave narrative.
4. English miners made up a significant portion of the population in southwest Wisconsin; most worked in lead mines.
5. Elsewhere in this issue, Bell noted that "We give this week a characteristic letter from this lady. We regret her recent illness, and hope her recovery is fully established."

Elevator 9 August 1873: 3
Mud Hill, Aug. 1, 1873

Mr. Editor,—"In the midst of councilors there is safety;" so says the good book,[1] and we must believe it. I have been sick, and truly have been in the midst of councilors, and can say if I am alive 'tis not due to the united wisdom of my councilors, but contrawise. I never thought until of late, that the world was so full of remedies, and all mankind, and especially womankind were physicians. Friend Bell, don't get sick, for you may have good digestion, but that will avail you nothing; there is all the mineral kingdom you must digest; all the roots and herbs, bitter and sweet, if burning with fire, you must have made into hot tea, and if freezing with chills, pounded ice on the head; if your head is hot, and the only comfortable part is your feet, mustard is put on to make them as hot as your head; and if perspiration starts instantly you are sweltered in blankets. No one physician can do all this; but just think—twenty people come in to see you in one week, and all of them with a sure remedy. You commence with the first—it is a compound of four or five of the bitterest herbs in botany, all cooked separate, then mixed with a certain amount of gin. One dose of that turns your stomach for twenty-four hours, and then the dogs can have it; but the dishes you cooked the herbs in, will the bitter never leave them. Several nice things you thought to relish are spoiled, and they are set one side. Next day you compound another prescription and find a mess so disgusting, that you wonder why you have no sense but a twinge of deadly pain; but the giver of the remedy says she was worse than you and was cured in three days, makes you take the nasty stuff— and lo, when three days are passed, you are ready to send for your physician, and go back to his drugs; knowing that in three days more you would have been well *forever*. Then the doctor wants to know what you have been doing, his medicine[s] don't have the desired effect; he then bleeds you, and when the thermometer is 104 in the shade, he applies tartar of antimony, to finish the burning the sun and fever have nearly completed. Oh! how you think of all the cool places you have known, the ice and snow, cool springs and deep wells. Then you wonder if the burnings of the condemned are worse, and when you feel that you are burned up you fall asleep to dream of falling in the burning pit; you wake and conclude to try a dear friend's remedy and so you go on, trying one specific after another, and find the great army of remedies is not half beaten, and your poor stomach is *hors de combat*; it will not retain even cold water and then comes in Doctor Common Sense and cries stop! stop! and you find you have stop'd none too soon; but your dear friends, whose remedies your poor stomach spurned, say you would not take their remedies, and of course, cannot expect to get well. Now Mr. Editor, don't get sick. If you want anything to eat you are told it is hurtful and you are given something you abhor, and told to eat it for it is good for you. Don't expect to use your teeth, for only spoon victuals are allowed, and gruel and broth your daily bill of fare. Mr. Trask says not one dish in the house, but is full of medicine, and he has bought new tin ware, as ours was too bitter for use, and now he wishes me to use his remedy, and I take kindly to the bread, meat and potatoes, but not the tobacco, which I class with the remedies of my friends, which failed to cure me because I would not take them.

—Semper Fidelis

1. From Proverbs 24:6–7, which reads, "For by wise counsel thou shalt make thy war, and in multitude of counselors there is safety. Wisdom is too high for a fool: he openeth not his mouth in the gate."

⌒

Elevator 30 August 1873: 2
Nevada City, Aug. 17, 1873

Mr. Editor,—I thought not to use my pen politically again, but I cannot refrain just this once, and after I will try and hold my peace. The Republican Convention, held here the 5th inst., indorsed [sic] Booth for Senator, and all the nominees of the Convention were pledged to his support.[1] They denounced George C. Gorham with railroad monopoly, Chinese immigration, etc.[2]

I am done with the party this year, and I am looking around to find consolation elsewhere. I can find no resting place among Democrats; they having the week before, in a Convention held here denounced Railroad monopoly, Chinese immigration, and Republican rule generally, I cannot see one iota of difference and I feel that the weakness of both parties is manifested, when they thus bring foreign issues in a state election. The Chinese question belongs to the general government, and the final solution will need great wisdom to dispose of and be true to the principles of our government. I am not afraid of Chinese (or the *Chronicle's* leprosy so prevalent in

San Francisco) but believe God will make plain our duty to them if we desire to do it, and I sincerely believe the same loving Father who has just brought us from oppression, now tries us by bringing us in contact with them; and how apparent the lesson we learned "to remember those in bonds as being bound with them."[3] So you see the anti-Chinese plank of the platform I don't endorse.

Railroad monopoly is the great scare-crow of to-day, I only wish from my heart we had the railroad monopoly and all here in Nevada City. Many years ago I lived in Illinois and no railroads were in operation in the State. People living 80 miles west of Chicago, loaded their wheat on wagons, and three days were passed on those long dreary roads, camping out by night, and often for hours fast in some muddy slough; and when in Chicago, fifty cents a bushel was counted a high price for grain. Many farmers came home after seven days absence with a barrel of salt, half a barrel of sugar, and half a barrel of dried apples, the value of 40 bushels of wheat, after the necessary expenses were taken out. By and by railroad talk began, then opposition began too. While some saw ease and prosperity, others feared their horses would be useless and only saw ruin. The first ten miles of the Railroad was built.[4] I remember one old farmer sold his wheat, left his team and rode in to Chicago on the cars, and was so delighted he came home, sold out team and all, saying he would travel on the cars hereafter. He moved to Cottage Grove Station[5]; and if he had remained two years longer on his old place, the cars would have passed his door daily. Well, the road at last reached the Mississippi river, property rose in value, lands improved, and people embarrassed with debts, and living in poor dwellings suddenly found themselves rich, built fine houses, and to-day no richer prosperous country can be seen than along the Chicago and Galena railroad; yet the hue and cry was no greater than those now against railroad monopoly. And while the Illinois railroad was being built, and they were selling lands (granted to them by government) to actual settlers, the same cry was heard, and yet thousands of the poor of both Europe and America were enabled to become land holders by the noble terms of the company, and the easy access to market by railroad. I traveled all through that country on horseback before the railroad was built, and I said many times when crossing prairies that seemed vast as the ocean, "no one will ever live here;" yet as soon as the road was built, settlers flocked in and dotted the broad prairies with school houses and churches as landmarks; while the pleasant homes, beaming fields of grain, orchards of fruit, "made the desert to blossom as the rose."[6]

That the Central Pacific Railroad is a blessing none can deny, and one Senator like George C. Gorham, who has manliness enough not to be a tool in the hands of politicians is worth more to us with his railroad propensity than a dozen like our gentle Governor who sees danger afar off on railroad monopoly.[7] I never had a free ride on the Central Pacific Railroad, and never expect to, yet when I am on that road I feel proud to live in an age and among people who could build it, and I feel that they ought to be rich and I ought to rejoice in their prosperity. So you see I don't endorse the anti-railroad resolution in the platform.

—Mrs. D. D. Carter

1. When Eugene Casserly (1820–1883), an Irish American who had served in the U.S. Senate as a California Democrat since 1869, announced that he would resign for medical reasons in 1873, a faction of the California Republican party attempted to push Governor Newton Booth (1825–1892) into the seat—over the objections of a range of groups. See Lauren E. Crane, ed., *Newton Booth of California: His Speeches and Addresses*.

2. On Gorham—including his pro-railroad and pro-Chinese stances—see notes to Carter's letter of 6 September 1867 in the 20 September 1867 *Elevator*.

3. Carter's views on the "Chinese question" are actually much more liberal than Bell's (or those of several African Americans), who fell victim to the same xenophobia that dominated many whites. Her stance may well have been shaped by interacting with members of Nevada County's large Chinese American population.

4. The Galena and Chicago Union Railroad was chartered in 1836, but active construction did not begin until 1848, when workers got as far as Oak Ridge (now the Chicago suburb of Oak Park). It was completed in 1853. See William Cranon, *Nature's Metropolis*.

5. Carter may be referring to the Cottage Grove that was then on the outer edge of Chicago.

6. Isaiah 35:1 says that "The wildness and the solitary place shall be glad for them, and the desert shall rejoice, and blossom as the rose."

7. Booth, famous as an orator, repeatedly attacked railroad monopolies.

⌒

Elevator 6 September 1873: 3
Nevada City, Aug. 21, 1873

Mr. Editor,—Having told you what I thought of the Chinese and anti railroad hobbies of this campaign, and the desire to elevate Booth to the Senatorship by the Republicans of Nevada county, just imagine my surprise to read in the *Chronicle* that it was a rebuke to Senator Sargent in his old home.[1] Now to the truth. Mr. Sargent had not offices enough to give every

Republican in this county one, and consequently there were lots of bolt-ers—sore-heads. Why an old Republican told me he would bolt and get an office for it; and last year went for Greely and has no office yet; and that is the opposition to Sargent.[2] That would not sound nice in Convention, so they draw in back pay and mining land law as terrible things demand-ing immediate action; and not one of these pledged to sustain Booth, and pledged in favor of those resolutions care one iota whether the mineral land law is modified or Sargent gives up his back pay; all that is wanted just now is something to talk about.

I hate milk and water people, and Mr. Editor, don't put it in my obit-uary, "left not an enemy behind;" for it would make me kick in my coffin. People who dare to speak what they believe to be the truth, regardless of the world's opinion like Geo. C. Gorham and Sargent, bless the world much more than smooth tongued polished lady-like gentlemen; and I for one sin-cerely hope Gorham will be Senator.[3] I cannot forget his brave utterances in our behalf, when the hiss of disapproval was heard and his standing up bravely to his words his ideas of brotherhood and enlarged humanity, so dif-ferent from this day and age makes him worthy of the Senatorial toga.

While the candidates are pledged to sustain Booth in this county, yet it is not safe for a colored voter to bolt; for we well know the Democrats will place Wallace in the position,[4] or someone like him, who is antagonistic to all efforts the colored people may make, and who so fear their superiority that they may say as did Senator O'Conner of Grass Valley[5]; "that if there was only one child of color in his district, and it must be educated, he would favor building a house and sustaining a school for it alone before admitting it in a white school." Brave words for an Irishman and Catholic, I hope no colored man will vote for him.[6] There are too many foreigners like him in America already, who claim more than the native born, and who talk and act in America like men, bred in halls of wealth and renown instead of hovels.

I am done with politics this year, and I do feel better for having had my say, and I only hope Gov. Booth will fail of election and Gorham will be elected, and the *Chronicle* will go on getting subscribers for their map, and let Sargent alone, and that the men elected this fall will be willing to grant equal school privileges to all children.

—Mrs. D. D. Carter

1. See Carter's 17 August 1873 letter in the 30 August 1873 *Elevator*. Aaron Augustus Sargent (1827–1887) was a U.S. senator from California between 1873 and 1879 and an ally of

George Gorham in the fight against Newton Booth. Sargent lived in Nevada City in the 1850s, and it is possible that he knew one or both of the Carters.

2. For basic information on Greeley, see notes to Carter's 6 May 1872 letter published in the 18 May 1872 *Elevator*.

3. For basic information on Gorham, see notes to Carter's 6 September 1867 letter published in the 20 September 1867 *Elevator*.

4. Probably William T. Wallace, a former Know-Nothing who was chief justice of the California Supreme Court from 1872 to 1879.

5. Probably Miles P. O'Connor, who represented Grass Valley in the state assembly at the beginning of the Civil War.

6. Another example of Carter's vehement prejudice against area Irish, which was likely the result of Irish racism and ties to the Democrats.

⌒

Elevator 29 November 1873: 2
Carson City, Nov. 21, 1873

Mr. Editor,—I shall not be able to tell you anything about Carson, as you visited there last spring and your admirable description I read with pleasure; yet after a sojourn of four weeks here I have seen and felt what you did not while here—the "Washoe Zephyrs."[1] I find Carson beautiful for situation, surrounded by mountains whose sides channeled, broken and abrupt brown and grey, make a formidable defence [sic] to the beautiful valley in which this city is located, and I can imagine no more pleasing picture in early spring when nature puts on her dress of green that this valley and city with its background of grey. When first settled here many of the mountain sides were clothed with timber, all has been peeled and consumed; now only sage brush is to be seen, except in inaccessible places stunted pines may be seen growing. Carson is a long city, also a level one. Carson street is the principal street, and I should judge is a mile in length with many fine buildings. Yet the rushing spirit of the Pacific Coast is apparent here, where building for the present and no heed for the future is taken, consequently many cheap buildings are to be seen now, when in a few years good substantial stone blocks will take their places. Already, some of the finest stone buildings on the Pacific Coast are erected here. One mile from the city is the State Prison, and near it is a quarry of granite, and the convicts are employed dressing stone, which makes the material cheap. In company with Mr. Grinage and Mrs. Bullock, I visited the Mint, machine shops of Truckee and Virginia City Railroad, the Capital and Orphan Home.[2] I think, Friend Bell, it would not do for me to visit a mint every day; money seems easily made. I should depreciate the coin; to see the trade dollar dropping from the dies like the clicking of a clock, would impress every one with the idea of safety in finance, and the bare possibility of financial crisis would seem preposterous while in the Carson Mint. We found the Lieutenant-Governor[3] on duty while in the mint—and of course I was pleased to see the notable, and still more pleased to hear his permission to see the coining done. We handled the money when warm, and gave it back with a slight regret, thinking of the words recorded in the great book—"the love of money is the root of all evil,"[4] and walked out of the mint impressed with the greatness of mind in perfecting machinery to make such perfect coins out of the gold and silver dug from the hills. Some have not doubted the future of Carson, or the great machine shops of the railroad would not have been built. I never saw finer buildings in my life built of cut granite. They will be as enduring as the mountains. When I saw their immense size I wondered, until I was told 28 trains departed daily. I think Carsonites have reason to be proud of their depot, the neatest and best I have seen on this coast, and I wondered why they would support an anti-railroad paper, when the railroad had done so much for their city. I learned that the Dolly Varden wave[5] which swept California had swamped Nevada also in the fall elections, and the Carson Daily *Appeal* had opposition in the *Tribune*, a semi weekly, devoted to the anti railroad anti subsidy political party. More soon.

—Mrs. D. D. Carter

1. Made famous by Mark Twain's *Roughing It* (1872), these gusts from the Sierra Nevada struck many, as they did Twain, as "peculiarly scriptural winds."

2. On Frederick Grinage, see notes to Carter's letter of 4 April 1869 published in the 9 April 1869 *Elevator* as well as the 1870 Census of Placer County, California, 459, and 1880 Census of Ormsby County, Nevada, 64D. Grinage's wife Rachel (c. 1848–?) was born in Pennsylvania. Frederick Grinage's cousin Rachel Bullock (c. 1820–?) was Maryland-born. Her husband (c. 1814–before 1880), whose first initial was "W," was a Kentucky-born laborer and gardener; their son Frederick (c. 1858–?) was likely named for Grinage and was born in California. See 1870 Census of Washoe County, Nevada, 467. Rachel and son are listed with the Grinage family in the 1880 Census.

3. Frank Denver (c. 1827–?) a Democrat, gained attention throughout the West when Nevada (and his boss, Governor Lewis Rice Bradley) decided to split the lieutenant governor's position from the role of warden of the state penitentiary and Denver initially refused to vacate the prison. Carter's visit to Carson City came soon after Denver was ejected, and so he was probably a bit of a tourist attraction.

4. 1 Timothy 6:10 reads, "which while some have coveted after, they have erred for the faith, and pierced themselves through with many sorrows."

5. The Dolly Vardens split away from California Republican Party along with leader and founder Governor Newton Booth. They took their name from a key character in Charles

Dickens's *Barnaby Rudge*—a spoiled flirt who captivated audiences and wore a trademark multicolored calico pattern. So popular was Dickens's character that her name was also given to a hat style, a rose, a type of trout, a waltz, and one of the earliest black women's baseball teams (out of Philadelphia).

~

Elevator 6 December 1873: 2
Carson City, November 26, 1873

Mr. Editor,—The State Capital is a true building, yet not imposing at first appearance, but when close to it you see it is beautifully proportioned and worthy of silver State.[1] It stands in the centre of a large square now uncultivated, but in time no doubt, will be filled with trees, shrubs and grass plots burdened with flowers.

We visited first the Governor's room and were introduced to his private secretary, who we found to be a gentleman in deportment; he insisted on us to look around, which we did cheerfully, noticing a large picture of Gov. Bradley; we remembered his face, having been on the cars when the Governor came abroad, before leaving the Capital; we met him; were introduced, shook hands and pronounced him Democratic in principle as well as politics.[2] He was courteous and treated us with all politeness.

We were introduced to deputy State Controller Theodore Hall,[3] and he showed his books, which we pronounce the neatest we ever saw—not one blemish about them—the handwriting looking like lady's work, so fine and perfect. He showed us his book of warrants, and if we had been entitled to one, we only would have had to step across the hall and enter into the State Treasurer's Department to have it cashed; and that there was no lack of money, we were assured when the door of the safe was opened to our view, and the gold twenties on trays seemed inexhaustible. The obliging treasurer asked me to lift one drawer full of them. I with my lame arm was obliged to decline. Fred[4] took hold and he was glad to soon give it back, or pretended he was; I know it was heavy to hold, but I think it would have been easy to handle.

We went through the Supreme Court rooms, State Library, State Geological and Mineralogical Cabinet; all the different rooms were furnished in fine style, and the carpets were beautiful. We went into the legislative halls and looked around, regret[t]ing that it was not in session. We brought our imagination into play, and had before us the very smart man who introduced the celebrated bill against miscegenation and we felt all the horror he did, only it was on the other side—we being filled with a great desire to present before the honorable body a bill compelling all white men to marry colored women, squaws and even China women who were mothers to their children, and so help to support and educate their own flesh and blood. Legislative and Senate halls were silent, only our brain was active.[5] We saw and admired the rooms, was pleased with the courteous reception shown us, and felt all was due Mr. Grinage who has been the gentleman while among them, and so merited respect.[6]

—Mrs. D. D. Carter

1. Construction began on the Nevada State Capitol building in 1870 and was completed the next year. Its prominent silver dome reminded residents and visitors of the booms that had led to statehood in 1864.
2. From Carter, of course, this is a bit of a backhanded compliment, as she disagreed vehemently with Bradley's politics.
3. I have not yet found biographical information on Hall.
4. Likely Frederick Grinage. On the Grinage family, see notes to Carter's letters of 4 April 1869 published in the 9 April 1869 *Elevator* and 21 November 1873 published in the 29 November 1873.
5. It is likely that Carter was referring to a bill "to prevent miscegenation" introduced on 14 February 1873 by Lincoln County assemblyman P. L. Shoaff; see Rusco, *Good Time Coming*, 79.
6. This treatment was probably due at least in part to Grinage's prominent place in Nevada's black community.

⌒

Elevator 13 December 1873: 2
Home, Mud Hill, Dec. 8, 1873.

Mr. Editor,—After a pleasant sojourn of five weeks in Carson, I am "home" again, invigorated in health, almost rejuvenated in mind, and strengthened in my conviction that the solicitude of friends alleviates the ills of life, and unites us in one common brotherhood. My visit was so agreeable, so filled with pleasing associations that I could weekly for an indefinite period give our readers of the ELEVATOR reminiscences of my visit to the "happy valley." I will not, however, satiate them, but I cannot refrain from occasionally giving an item. My contribution will this week be

The Orphan's Home.[1]

This a fine building, two stories in height; it stands in the centre of a large square, the land of which is under cultivation and yields the vegetables consumed by the inmates. A nice gravel walk from the street to the front door, and on the side, flower beds makes it look home-like, and inside it is the picture of neatness. The lower story is divided into reception room, parlor, dining and school rooms, kitchen, hat, coat and wash rooms. The upper story is arranged into sleeping apartments. There are thirty orphans, and among them one little colored girl, and no distinction is shown. In fact, Mr. Editor, Carson is head and shoulders above us in many things, and in this matter of equality before the law they are all right. It did my soul good to see our children going with the white children to the same schools, and to see their names on their roll of honor. Every department of the public schools has colored children in it and the war of races, which so many prophesied and desired to see has not been seen, but contrawise all is harmony. What a pity Casserly[2] could not go to the Carson school and learn something; there is where he ought to be; 'tis well he resigned his seat in the Senate of the United States. Read his reason for not supporting Governor Booth for Senator.[3]

Churches.

Carson has several fine churches and great ministerial talent. The Rev. Mr. Fisher, State Superintendent of Public Instruction preaches for the Methodists.[4] I have heard him pronounced the Beecher of the Pacific Coast,[5] and I think he is entitled to that honor; he has enlarged Christian views, a cultivated mind, ready delivery united to great zeal; and a frail body holds an over energetic spirit. Rev. Mr. Woods of the Presbyterian church is also an interesting speaker.[6] His sermons are full of metaphors, flowery and pleasing, and yet inculcating good morals and sound theology. The Rev. Mr. Beard (colored) supplies Virginia City and Carson, preaching for the A.M.E. Church.[7] The membership is small. I heard him once. He is an earnest speaker.

The colored people in Carson seem to be all doing well, have pleasant homes, and with the school advantages their children have, I think they ought to be happy.

Surprise Party

I am under obligation to my friends for a very pleasant surprise party. Mrs. Stedmier and Miss Mary Young were the principals in getting up the surprise, and they were ably assisted by the colored people in Carson.[8] The table was as fine as ever I saw—set out with silver and glass, it shone like Aladdin's palace, while it fairly groaned beneath the weight of turkeys, chickens, cakes, pies, candies, fruit and nuts; wine in abundance, too.

Clear Creek Canyon.

I enjoyed a very pleasant ride with Colonel Johnson, and I feel that the Alps of Switzerland afford no finer scenery than I saw while riding up Clear Creek Canyon.[9] When the mountains were made, I think no canyon was there; but a mighty convulsion of nature, and they were rent in twain, and left the deep gully between the hills just wide enough for a road, and, towering on either side, lofty mountains, with huge boulders fashioned into every conceivable shape. There were castles more grand than any on the Rhine, with casement and towers, loop-holes and guns, and when twilight came, out came the soldiers, clad in armor. I imagined I could see the frowns open their faces to see us driving by their castles, strong without a retinue of retainers, and as twilight settled into darkness, I saw them walking on their walls, and I thought of all the legends I had read, of all the ghost stories I had heard, and I can assure you I was glad when Clear Creek Canyon was behind us, and we were in the beautiful valley nearing the city.

To Mr. Grinage and his sister, Mrs. Lee, his cousin, Mrs. Bullock, all who cared for me in my hours of pain and did so much for me, I am under lasting gratitude, and I pray my Heavenly Father to shower down blessings upon them; and I shall always feel a warm interest in the two boys, Freddie Bullock and Eddie Lee, whom I learned to love, and who faithfully ministered to my comfort for five weeks, always doing cheerfully whatever I asked them to do.[10] May they be kept from evil, and at last be on the grand roll of honor when the Judge shall make up his jewels.

Thanksgiving dinner with Mr. Lawrence and family, Mr. Lane and family, Mr. Grinage, sister and cousin as guests; we had turkey, pumpkin pie, mince pie, oysters fresh from Baltimore, champagne and other wines, and much more. I left the dinner table for the depot, where I bid good-bye to Miss Young, Mrs. Bullock and Mr. Grinage.[11]

—Mrs. D. D. Carter.

1. Only recently opened—the first child was admitted in October 1870—the Nevada State Orphan's Home on Carson City's Fifth Street was built at a cost of $8500 and heralded as an important innovation. It burned down in 1902.
2. Eugene Casserly (1820–1883), an Irish American who served in the U.S. Senate as a California Democrat from 1869 until he resigned for medical reasons in 1873. See notes to Carter's 17 August 1873 letter in the 30 August 1873 *Elevator*.
3. Casserly did work for a time with Booth, though the two seem to have split.
4. Albert N. Fisher (c. 1839–?), a well-known minister who served a term as the Nevada school superintendent; he is mentioned a number of times in Rusco, *Good Time Coming*.
5. A reference to Henry Ward Beecher (1813–1887), known across the nation for his powerful sermons.
6. I have not yet been able to identify "Mr. Woods."
7. I have not yet been able to identify "Mr. Beard," though he is briefly mentioned in Rusco, *Good Time Coming*.
8. Wife of Nelson Sturdmeyer (c. 1828–?; sometimes spelled Stedmier, sometimes spelled Stoudenmire, etc.), Rose Stedmier was born in the South (either Georgia or Virginia) c. 1828. The couple had one son, David, born in California or Nevada, c. 1853. See 1870 Census of Carson City, Nevada, 255, and 1880 Census of Carson City, Nevada, 50D. I have not yet identified "Miss Young." The black community of Carson City was relatively small.
9. I have not yet identified "Colonel Johnson." Clear Creek Canyon is just outside of Carson City.
10. On Bullock, see Carter's letter of 21 November 1873 published in the 29 November 1873 *Elevator*. Edward S. Lee (c. 1860–?) was the Maryland-born son of Mary J. Lee (c. 1820–?), also Maryland-born, who seems to have had a relationship to the Grinage/Bullock family, as she and her son were living with them in 1880. See 1880 Census of Ormsby County, Nevada, 64D. Also see Carter's dedication to her 1873 Christmas story in the 20 December 1873 *Elevator*.
11. I have not yet identified "Mr. Lawrence." "Mr. Lane" is probably John Lane (c. 1831–?), a Virginia City cook who had been born in the West Indies; see 1870 Census of Storey County, Nevada, 442.

⌒

Elevator 20 December 1873: 3

A Christmas Story

Dedicated to Masters Freddie Bullock and Eddie Lee,[1] by their friend, Mrs. D. D. Carter

Three Ways of Accumulating Wealth

William Sheffer, Truman Wilkins and Orin Beard were three boys nearly of an age.[2] I can recollect them, when the eldest was not more than twelve years old, and that one was William. I can see him to-day as he looked then, tall and with awkward way, which denoted bashfulness; bright eyes that were always twinkling like stars, yet he had a look about him that made all say "a smart boy," and I thought, when looking at his curly head, what a handsome boy. I was a little girl of six years, and I said to grandma when we were alone, ain't he handsome? "Handsome he who handsome does," she said. I saw him many times during the next two years, and he always seemed to me to grow handsomer each time I saw him; and during that time daily his mother rehearsed in my hearing his wonderful feats of scholarship; he was always at the head of his class; he had done every sum of Dabell's arithmetic,[3] and so smart was he that an uncle promised to send him to Dartmouth college, when he was old enough. His mother said he was anxious to go, and his desire for education was that he might become rich, for nothing else did he talk about, and he said he wanted money when young, he did not intend to wait until he was old and grey. When he was fifteen a family moved into the place who assumed great style, and who had two sons, who were soon intimate friends of William. I have not told you that William was very susceptible of outside influence, easily won over to do as others wished, and two or three times, he had been detected in doing mischievous acts, but to his mother he steadily denied it, and she poor soul, believed him the embodiment of truth; and if a mother has to lose faith in a child how hard it is. I can remember that mother's look (all these years) when one morning she came to my grandmother with her eyes full of tears, and told her that William had told a lie, and she knew it, and yet her excuse was the influence the Meade boys with whom he had become intimate. Now his whole desire was to do as they did, and games were their pastimes. Cards they handled like experts, and they represented to William that money could be made easier and quicker by cards than by hard work; so his studies were neglected, he never went to college, but when he was 21 years and 3 months old, my father who was Sheriff took him to Auburn State Prison for robbery.[4] Four years he was there, when he died, and on a beautiful Christmas day his body brought from prison to his childhood home was borne from his mother's house to a grave.

Truman Filkins[5] never knew his parents. When he was three years old Mr. Filkins took him from the poor house, and I think he never missed a mother's love, for Mrs. Filkins was one of the best and dearest old ladies who ever lived, and Truman, when I first saw him was a rosy-cheeked boy of eight years. We used to play together, and I often left my dolls in his care, when grandma called me from play. I many times told him he was not half as handsome as William, and he always laughed. I cannot remember once of his being angry all the years I knew him. I can recollect that he was always talking of riches, and when I first knew him he wanted to be rich to buy Ma' Filkins a silk dress; when older to buy a horse for Pa' Filkins, and in a year or two more he wanted to be rich, to open a store; and many a promise of candy did I have when he opened his store. His companion at home was an invalid sister, two years older than himself; she never walked, having fallen from the arms of her nurse when an infant and injured her spine. She had a chair with wheels, and on bright sunny days she would sit in the open air and watch our play. I remember she often chided him, because he did not love study, and often told him how smart William was, and urged him to try and be like him; but no, Truman was dull and stupid; he seemed likely to remain so, as far as books were concerned. About the time William began his evil associations Mr. Filkins moved away on a farm; after that I often heard of him as the little farmer, among his horses, cows and poultry. Before he was twenty his dear adopted parents had both died, and left him to care for Amanda, the helpless sister; and so much confidence did Pa' Filkins have in him that he willed all his property to him, and I read that will, and this is what it said: "To Truman, my beloved adopted son, I give and bequeath all my personal property, real estate, and to his loving care I bequeath my dear afflicted child, Amanda, believing he will do for her as I have done for him, having this confidence in him because he never told an untruth, never use[d] profane language, nor drank intoxicating drinks." Faithful to his trust, slowly but surely accumulating wealth, he lived sensible, and the world spoke of him as a good man; by and by as a rich man, and all sorrowed when he lost his life, when the steamer "Swallow" was destroyed on the Hudson River.[6] Trying to save his sister they both found death together; and the poor children of his native town every Christmas have a fine dinner provided by his will.

Orin Beard was an only child. His father was a rich man, the owner of a large cotton mill, and so proud was he of his wealth and his son, that he thought no one good enough to associate with his boy, but Orin like all boys would have his playmates; and how much better for parents to choose good children for companions for their own, than to leave them to pick up with their childish fancies any one. I remember one day, Mr. Beard came to grandmother's after Orin, and found William and Truman there. The three boys were playing together; he took Orin roughly by the arm and asked him

if he was not ashamed to play with a poor house brat. Grandma told him
to close his mouth for very shame, and with an ominous shake of the head
said: "Curses like chickens, come home to roost."7 Orin always was ready
to talk of riches, and was as desirous to gain them as though his father
was poor. I can remember his telling me he would build a mill twice as
large as his father's when he was a rich man. As a child he was penurious,
never divided anything; as far as study went he was medium, and I do not
think his parents cared for him to excel in anything, he was their boy and
that to them was all. I know it was said that they did not eat good victuals,
they wanted to increase their wealth for Orin. I can look back now, and
see Mr. Beard walking about with a sheep's grey cloth coat; for ten years
I never saw him wear anything else, and to ask him for charity was worth
one's life. One cold Christmas night, a stranger stop'd at his place and
asked to stop over night; he drove him from his door. Orin grew up in that
atmosphere, and it is not strange that his title when not twenty one years
old was "Stingy-Beard." His parents saved and starved for him until they
could do it no longer, and his mother died; the father was bed-ridden, and
Orin feared he would live too long, took him to the overseers of the poor
house—they sent him back with his helpless father, and the old man died
from exposure. It was said then, grandma told me that his mother died in the
poor house. I saw Orin in 1853, in the Insane Asylum at Utica, N.Y., where he
was catching flies—the richest man in the asylum.8 Now, which way will my
boys grow rich. I hope not at the sacrifice of truth or honor, but rich in good
works.

---

1. On Bullock, see Carter's letter of 21 November 1873 published in the 29 November 1873
   Elevator, as well as her 8 December 1873 letter in the 13 December 1873 *Elevator*. On Lee,
   see Carter's 8 December 1873 letter in the 13 December 1873 *Elevator*.
2. I have not yet been able to identify these figures.
3. *Dabell's Schoolmaster's Assistant* by Nathan Dabell went through several editions in the early
   nineteenth century.
4. This is one of the few descriptive references Carter makes to a father, and this father's service
   as sheriff would seem to contradict the report of injuries done to him given in Carter's "My
   Aunt Sybel" published in the 5 March 1869 *Elevator*. I have not yet been able to determine
   whether this figure is fictionalized or not. The New York State Prison in Auburn, Cayuga
   County, was built in 1816.
5. No explanation is given for the switch from "Wilkins" in the initial sentence of this story to
   "Filkins" for the rest of the tale.
6. The *Swallow*, based out of Troy, New York, was built in 1836 and hit a rock, caught fire,
   and sank in the Hudson River on 7 April 1845. Between fifteen and twenty were killed. See
   Frederick Erving Dayton, *Steamboat Days*, Chapter 4.

7. A line from "The Curse of Kehama," by Robert Southey (1774–1843).
8. The New York State Lunatic Asylum opened in 1843 and was directed by innovator Amariah Brigham in the 1850s.

⌒

Elevator 7 March 1874: 2
Home, Feb. 22, 1874.

Mr. Editor,—In wonder at my long silence, and especially at this time when the school question is the absorbing theme of pen and tongue. While many were disappointed on the vote of Mr. Cowdery's bill,[1] I was not; and again, I did not feel bad at the result. It will not hurt us, but them; and years hence, those who voted nay, will try in vain to get the opprobrium from their names. Yes! in vain, just as the trustees of the Livingston fund; for of all the wrongs perpetrated on the colored people of the Pacific Coast, the disposition of that fund was the greatest.[2] Friend Bell, I feel just as bad over that transaction as when we talked the matter over at Mud Hill, and have looked in vain to see some use made of that rod you had in pickle for them, and while I have no personal enmity to one of the trustees, I do feel that they might just as well have dug up the bones of Starr King and sold them for their own profit, as to appropriate money set apart for an object so sacred.[3] And at this time how much influence would have been gained to our cause by the erection of that school building; and again the school would have drawn pupils from every part of the coast, and rendered all the talent visible, for as it is now, many of our best minds who will not be brought in contact with the cosmopolitan world, will never be half developed.

Six months before the trustees (or a part of them) sent out their circular announcing the giving up, I saw Mr. Briar and had a long talk [with] him; he told me the money should never be diverted from the original intention, said he was determined the school building should be erected as soon as the sum had accumulated to $10,000.[4] Then judge of my surprise to see so soon after a grand surrender. I have waited now a long time to see the whole thing in print, the final settlement with all moneys paid; and trustees who have managed the thing owe it to the public to make a full statement. I fully believe they will have to answer to God for a lack of duty, and all the extenuation for their conduct so far has been too thin to satisfy conscientious men

and women; and if they have not fully given their reasons for their conduct
it is high time they did. You know friend Bell, it is easier to say kind things,
to agree with all, yet it is necessary some should say harsh things and true,
and while I may seem severe only in the fear of God have I written this.

—Semper Fidelis

1. Jabez F. Cowdery, who was a Republican state assemblyman from 1873 to 1875 and again
   from 1880 to 1881, introduced a bill to ban racial segregation in California schools in the
   wake of the state Supreme Court's decision in *Ward v. Flood*, a case that held separate
   schools just. The bill was narrowly defeated, even though Cowdery gave an impassioned
   speech—much of which was reprinted in the *Elevator*.
2. By this point, all hope of the Livingstone Institute—planned to be the first black secondary
   school in California—had evaporated; trustees promised for years to return donations to
   subscribers without following through. See Carter's 23 February 1873 letter published in the
   1 March 1873 *Elevator*.
3. On Starr King, who was one of the original directors of the Livingstone Institute committee
   before his untimely death, see notes to Carter's 4 July 1868 letter in the 10 July 1868 *Elevator*.
4. Reverend James Welch Brier (1814–1898), an Ohio-born Methodist minister who had ties to
   the Kansas Jayhawkers, was one of the white trustees of the Livingston Institute (originally,
   there were six white trustees and six black). His 1849 trip to California—from Galesburg,
   Illinois, across Death Valley is described in Gwinn Harrir Heap, *Central Route to the Pacific*.
   See also 1860 Census of Santa Clara County, California, 475; 1870 Census of Solano
   County, California, 85; 1880 Census of Nevada County, California (Grass Valley), 127D.

⌒

Elevator 14 November 1874: 3
Home, November 8, 1874.

Mr. Editor,—"How strange it is that the colored people South voted the
Democratic ticket." So said a man to me last week after reading the election returns from Louisiana, and rehearsing that old threadbare story of the
gratitude due the Republican party from the negro and telling me one thing
I never heard of before, that General Grant was entirely devoted to the
negro, and to the entire seclusion of the white race. Now, Mr. Editor,
I come before your readers to say I am sick of politics and politicians, and yet
this election with its Democratic victory seems the natural result to me of
neglect on the part of Republicans towards the colored people. The failure
to pass the "Civil Rights Bill," lost the Southern States to the Republicans,
and if they are not willing to concede this truth now the time will come

when they will acknowledge it.[1] I am heartily tired of hearing the *Gratitude* story commented on in this city. One year ago, many old time Republicans voted the Democratic ticket. Why[,] a man whom they did not like received the nomination for State Senator and every Sargent man bolted (by the way several of them are in San Francisco holding government offices now).[2] What had they at stake? Why[,] bread and butter; some of them and all of them feared their leaders' disapproval and they bolted and voted and elected Mr. O'Connor, (Senator)[3]; a man whose every act and vote during his political record has been antagonistic to Republicanism; a man who voted against every amendment; and these intelligent Republicans voted for him and now they talk so loud of the *ingratitude* of the ignorant negroes; who standing with death all around them, their wives and little ones murdered before their faces, houses burned, hunted like wild beasts, many of them losing faith in God, who through long years of slavery never once doubted their deliverance, but with child-like trust watched and waited—now when ruin and death around them what shall they do? Think you, we should not lose faith in the Republican party when we saw we were unprotected, and be ready for the tempter, who with fair speech would promise safety in the future? And the thought of peace and rest where one has lived and buffeted, as many of these poor souls have been for years was enough to make many of them vote as the paper say "openly the Democratic ticket." While I regret the course taken, I could not say as a man said to me, "the negro has ruined the country," and class the Irishman and negro together; for the negro did not carry New York for the Democrats, while the Irish to a man voted for old Democracy[4]; and while politics and politicians are so rotten I see just such sweeping victories alternating between both Republican and Democrat; and I wait and hope our people may rise above their surroundings, and learn to trust one another more, for the just want of unity among ourselves works more harm than a hundred Democratic victories.

—Semper Fidelis.

1. Initially proposed by Senator Charles Sumner (1811–1874) and Representative Benjamin Butler (1818–1893) in 1870, this bill did not become law until 1875 (the Civil Rights Act of 1875; 18 Stat. 335). Guaranteeing equal treatment in public accommodations, conveyances, and services, it was overturned by the U.S. Supreme Court in 1883, paving the way for the decision in *Plessy v. Ferguson* (1896).
2. On Aaron A. Sargent, see notes to Carter's 21 August 1873 letter published in the 6 September 1873 *Elevator*.

3. Probably Miles O'Connor of Grass Valley; see notes to Carter's 21 August 1873 letter
   published in the 6 September 1873 *Elevator*.
4. Part of Carter's longstanding animosity toward Irish Americans.

⌒

Elevator 5 December 1874: 3
Home, Nov. 20, 1874.

Mr. Editor,—I have come to the conclusion that insecurity is everywhere
apparent, and however we may be situated we find that feeling always present, although 'tis augmented by surroundings. The theatre in our city is
believed by two thirds of the people dwelling here to be unsafe, and yet night
after night they go there. I have been there, and while listening to eloquence
have had this sense of insecurity intrude itself so quickly and painfully upon
me as to lose all interest in the speaker, and I seemed to be walking on my
own grave. You will say that was the extreme of insecurity, and at the time
this political parties are like our theatre; and while thousands of Republicans have gone over to the Democracy; this unsafe, insecure feeling is every
where predominant; neither party having confidence in the other; and
to-day if questioned, every Republican who voted with the Democrats
would say, I have not a shadow of faith in their principles only in the reforms
promised; and eight there is the insecurity; these renegade Republicans have
not impressed the Democrats with their stability—no, on the other hand
there is study long and deep to hold them for a purpose, and that purpose is
the next Presidential election which is now the absorbing thought of all. To
keep and hold them as Democratic voters requires great statesmanship for
some planks in the old building will have to be removed, some timbers loos-
ened and every one makes the old fabric more and more insecure.

Here are a few of the timbers and planks which will have to be loos-
ened—an unqualified acknowledgement of the amendments to the Constitution and Civil Rights; and what a queer looking thing Democracy would
be with Negro suffrage inscribed on their banner, when leading Democrats
say there is no condition for the negro but slavery, and their aim is to rein-
state, and yet to get and hold the colored vote until after the next Presidential election is their great study, and to hold their own platform with so
many planks removed.

There was a time when the unterrified speaker would open his lips and nigger would pop out; all knew him then as a sound Democrat and Democrats felt no insecurity. Now, listen and hear him talk of colored voters walking in solid phalanx voting the Democratic ticket. Oh! what a soul sickness comes over me; the rotten old building kept together by bad Republicans and bad colored voters. Lord help them, for they have gone in that building to be helplessly crushed to be a by-word for future generations; some ignorantly, and some from cupidity, and they have only rendered greater their insecurity.

—Semper Fidelis

Elevator 19 December 1874: 3

CHRISTMAS STORY[1]

To Mary Cobb Fullerton of Ohio[2] this Christmas Story is dedicated by Mrs. D. D. Carter, Christmas, 1874.

"We are come from the mountains of the old Granite state,
Where the hills are so lofty, magnificent and great."

How many thousands have heard the Hutchinsons sing those lines[3] and how many have thought how beautiful those hills and mountains were to inspire those singers, give them not only such sweet voices, but such enlarged ideas of humanity as to make them willing to sing for rich or poor, bond and free; and many may have thought that the State that gave them birth could not rear a son or daughter to disgrace their patrimony. In this earth's fairest spots will be found those who worship self alone and nothing good, true or beautiful in their surroundings can deter them from wrong.

Many years ago there lived in the "Old Granite State" a man by the name of Cobb who had two sons whom he tried to bring up in Godly fear, and to both he gave a good education. The eldest son, when twenty one years old left home and went to sea, and his parents never saw him again; for year after year passed and no message came from the wanderer, and at last aged

and grey, the father and mother went to the grave bequeathing the homestead to their youngest son, who was married and had two daughters and
one son, whose life passed happily with his sisters and parents, until manhood came to enfold him with an unfading crown of martyrdom.

When this young man was eighteen he was invited to visit western
New York, by a maternal uncle, who had settled in the village of Castile,
Wyoming County, (it was at that time Genesse County) and during the
summer vacation (for he was a student at Dartmouth College) he made the
visit and there met the lady who four years after became his wife. Soon after
he returned home he was surprised one day to be called to the door to greet
a stranger, and to his utter astonishment to be greeted affectionately in the
name of cousin. After wonderment came full explanation and then it was
known that the long mourned son of the grandfather was living and well,
and all these years had been growing rich; and having a family of children
he determined to send his eldest son to old Dartmouth, and to his neglected
kindred to form their acquaintance. It was soon known why this unnatural
son had kept all knowledge of himself from the old ones at home, but why
at last he had sent his son from Alabama to the old Granite State was never
fully understood. I have, in thinking of this matter come to the conclusion
that in his old age all his childhood with its purity came again through
memory to torture his soul with longings for the dear neglected ones and to
have his son imbibe some of the old Granite principles; such it seemed to me
to have been the reason for again making himself known through his son.

Now I leave all the rest and come to the story which has only to do
with the two cousins, Allen and John Cobb. Time flies swiftly, and yet to
the young it seems everything is lengthened out, and three years of college
life seem fully six to Allen and John,[4] and yet they passed less weariedly to
Allen who spent his vacation with his relations in the South, while John was
helping his parents on the old homestead. Let not the reader think for one
moment that there was unanimity of sentiment between these young men,
that the subject of slavery was never discussed. Allen was what his mother
admired, a fire eater,[5] and in temper almost ungovernable, and was only saved
from expulsion from college by his mild and strong minded cousin; and
I have been told that John's love towards Allen was apparent to every one
with whom they came in contact. Often was John seen to step in between his
cousin and other students to receive the blows, and his manly courage would
disarm the opponent; and moreover Allen was indebted to John for perfect
recitations in his studies. Every vacation did Allen importune John to go

South with him and become acquainted with his parents and see the work-ings of slavery and a promise was exacted when Allen's final leave-taking, that John alter his marriage, spend the winter with his bride on the Southern plantation, and if pleasant make it their permanent home.

The sun never rose over truer hearts than John Cobb and Alice Kellogg.[6] I wish I could take the readers of the ELEVATOR to the home of Alice in that beautiful valley in Western New York. Many years have passed since I saw it, and I was but a child, yet the quiet beauty of that cultivated home, which time has not with its cares and sorrows and joys faded from my memory. The house standing in a beach grove which sloped to the bank of the river on which Alice was at home in her skiff, and no doubt to-day many gray haired women are alive who enjoyed a row with her. The only and the eldest child— she was so dear to those parents who had spared nothing to make her truly great and good and worthy of the man to whom she had given her heart. And right royally they looked on that September morning when adieus were said, and they went first to Old Granite State and from there to Alabama.

Have you not often thought dear reader that this world would be far nicer if no one said harsh things, never reproved when necessary, if they had heard wrong, smile and pass on. There are many, yet, the majority who do just so, others like true heroes, count the cost and speak against wrong. Those are our moral surgeons who sever the limb that the body may live. In the second day's fighting at Gettysburg, among the wounded brought in was a little boy with his right arm shattered—nearly torn off by a ball. He was laid on a cot awaiting the surgeon, when the chaplain seeing his child face, went to him, talked and finally prayed for him, thinking he must soon die. When he ceased praying, the dear little drummer-boy looked at him and said, "you pray almost as good as mother, but I want to see the doctor." "Why, my little fellow, the surgeon will take off your arm and give you great pain," said the chaplain. "Yes, I know that," spoke the little hero, "but with-out I suffer great pain I shall die." The surgeon took off the arm and Ben-nie Corbett[7] lived to go home to Illinois to his mother, and again listen to her prayers. Now the one who dares to speak even if pain is caused, is truly a moral hero, and the world has in all ages been blessed by just such heroes; many whose lives have been written, and many who have died and left no record behind them; yet the principles they unflinchingly bear witness to have in the end been triumphant.

Judge the feelings of John and Alice when they learned the fact near their uncle's home in Alabama, that his great wealth had been gained by buying and selling human beings, and he had been what was known as a "nigger trader"—a being despised even among slave owners at the South in slavery's palmy days. I heard her say she did not close her eyes to sleep the night after learning that fact, but John and herself made a solemn vow to God never by word, deed, or silence to give sanction to slavery and made their visit and return to the North. A planter living a short distance from his uncle wished to get a tutor for his sons and John concluded to teach them for three months, and so lengthen out his means, for economy was a Granite principle and a part of his being. His employer was a gentle, good man, and treated his slaves with humanity, and often talked with John about the enormity of slavery, and said it was a curse to the county, and the [curse] included on the whites was fully as bad as on the blacks, and that his desire was to instil[l] right principles in his boys, but he found it uphill work, where every one was against him and he also said that the different planters thought and spoke ill of him, saying his influence was bad on their servants, as he treated them so well.

Christmas week, the yearly jubilee of the slaves, John and wife were to spend with the uncle's family, and to make their visit pleasant a great many were invited, and the large mansion was full of guests, and the Christmas dinner was a triumph of skill. Alice told me she never saw anything half as nice before, and that the table was laid for fifty guests. When all were seated, the name of the planter was mentioned, and his humanity called in question; one after another commented on his views in regard to slavery, and all spoke of him as worthy only of the hangman's rope, and John's uncle said he must be driven out of the State. Then John rose and with his great soul looking out of his eyes, and taking for his text these words of Jesus, "Blessed are the merciful for they shall obtain mercy,"[8] he preached to them, speaking in terms of joy of his friend whom all were against, and to his uncle, citing the example of his parents in glory, and reminding him of the old Granite principles he had forsaken, and said that "may God deal with me, as I deal with the oppressed!" Just then he fell dead, shot through the heart by his cousin Allen. Alice, broken-hearted, came home to dwell with her parents, and her little daughter born in the land of freedom was a consolation to them all, and while visiting her I learned this sad story, hoping she may be blessed with all good from our father in heaven.[9]

1. In the issue previous to this, Bell had offered the following notice: "OUR CHRISTMAS STORY.—We will next week commence an original Christmas Story, by our versatile

contributor, Mrs. D. D. Carter (Semper Fidelis) of Nevada City. In a private note, Mrs. Carter says the incidents are strictly true."

2. Although I have located a number of Mary Fullertons, I have not yet determined which is the one cited in the dedication.

3. These lines are from "The Old Granite State," by John Hutchinson (1821–1908), one of the famed abolitionist singing group, the Hutchinson Family Singers, who toured widely in the North; see Carol Brink, *Harps in the Wind*.

4. Neither Allen nor John Cobb appear in any of the alumni records for Dartmouth.

5. A term for proslavery extremists—generally applied to Southerners who urged secession well before Lincoln's election.

6. I have not yet found biographical material on Alice Kellogg, although there was a large Kellogg family in Genesse County, New York, during this period.

7. Bennie Corbett is not listed in the National Park Service's database of Civil War soldiers and sailors, and does not show up in a number of other similar sources.

8. Matthew 5:7, one of the beatitudes.

9. The Mary Cobb Fullerton of the dedication would seem to be the "little daughter" mentioned here.

Appendix A

Contributions to the *Christian Recorder*

Jennie Carter published only two short pieces—both under the penname "Semper Fidelis"—in the *Christian Recorder*, the Philadelphia-based organ of the African Methodist Episcopal Church. In so doing, she joined the company of black women ranging from Julia Collins to Frances Ellen Watkins Harper who appeared in the *Recorder*'s pages. Her first contribution, published in the 9 October 1869 issue, was well received: in the next issue, the editors noted that Carter's cover letter had said "If it pleases you, I will continue to write"; they responded, "Of course it pleases us, and we will be only too happy to give her room." In addition to commending her piece to "all mothers and teachers especially," the *Recorder* let readers know that Bishop Thomas M. D. Ward said the writings of "Semper Fidelis" were "at once original, spicy, and interesting." Still, the *Recorder*'s ads published in early 1870 not only listed "Semper Fidelis" as a contributor, but also identified her as "Mrs. D. D. Carter." Whether this unveiling surprised or troubled Carter is not yet known, but she published only one additional piece in the *Recorder*.

Christian Recorder 9 October 1869

GRANDMOTHER
Home Nook, Cal., Sept. 12th, 1869.

"I have told you his faults, now I will tell you his virtues," said a mother to me one day when she came with her boy to put him in my school. After listening to her long list of vices, in my heart I despised of being able to give my consent for James Richards[1] to remain as a pupil of mine. But one thing she said to me changed my resolve to one of eagerness to have him remain with me. "He never spoke a cross word to Grandmother," said the mother [. Nonetheless,] James was a bad boy. His record was bad. He had been expelled from the public school. His associates were the worst boys in town. He was untruthful, and had been detected pilfering. All this the mother told me, and more, and I had known it a long time, but I did not know until that day that he "always spoke kind to his Grandmother." He was to commence his studies the next morning. I assigned him tasks, but look at him when I would, I could not see him looking on his books. I said pleasantly to him, "James, is it hard work to study?" "No," he said gruffly. When the time of recitation drew near, I said, "James, please study, it is nearly time to recite." Not one question of his lessons could he answer. When school was dismissed I placed my hand kindly on his head and said "James, you have a grandmother. I had one once; she has been dead many years, and I loved her very much; now tell me about your Grandma?" "She is the best woman that ever lived," and oh! how his face brightened as he spoke. For two hours we talked about our grandmothers, his on earth, mine in heaven. That conversation made us friends [and] gave me the key to all that was unsolved in the boy. I knew the only way to reach his heart was through the "Dear Old Granny," as he called her, and I told him to "study hard through the week, and on Saturday we would visit his Grandmother." Study he did, and, if I thought at any time he was losing his interest in his books, I had only to say, "James, remember our visit," and his eyes would sparkle, a smile creep over his face, and then to his books with eagerness. On Saturday morning very early we started, for we had two miles to walk, and the day was warm.

Today how pleasant seems that walk, although more than twenty long years have passed since then, and I can hear the birds singing just as sweet as they sang then, but the dear boy who unfolded so much of his bitter life that day is not, I trust, singing in glory the song of Redeeming Love, which even the angels cannot sing. When we arrived at the house where "Granny" lived, James sprung from my side, and in the door he almost flew. I looked in a few moments after, and he was leading "Granny" by the hand towards me, who welcomed me in, and then laid her hand on my head and blessed me, and I feel that her benediction has followed me all these years. That day I learned that children may become martyrs. "Granny" told me that James' father was a drunkard, and many nights had she rose from her bed at midnight to let the boy in, and found him bleeding and bruised, with his life saved by flight; for in his drunken sprees the father's wrath always fell on James. I learned that the school children had taunted him with being a "Drunkard's brat," and he fought them, and was expelled, and I learned that all his vices were the fruits of that father's love for strong drink. In the boy's hunger he had stolen, and to avoid detection he had lied. "Dear Old Granny" said "he never told her an untruth." He was a pupil of mine for three years, and a more honest, truthful boy I never taught, and he told me if I had not taken him when his mother came with him, he would have run away and went to sea.

Grandmother and James are both at rest. The many prayers were heard and answered, for no one I have ever known died more respected and beloved than James Richards, who never spoke cross to his Grandmother.

—Semper Fidelis

1. I have not yet determined which of the myriad of James Richardses this refers to.

Christian Recorder 16 April 1870

True Pearls
Home Nook, Cal., March 18, 1870.

I am an old woman, and yet things that were told to me in childhood, I can remember, and many things that I know were false, have exercised an influence upon me, all through the years until now, and when I hear parents telling their children untruths, I tremble for the future of those children, and it matters not what the motive may be in the mind of the parent, it is always wrong to tell an untruth. Oh, if only mothers would cease to terrify their children into obedience, and remember that "love has readier will than fear."[1]

The conjuring up of a horrible image in the mind of an imaginative child, is fearful in its effects, and "the naughty man that will come after dark"[2] had made cowards of many children and embittered a long life, for it is impossible to get rid of those impressions. They influence us even while reasoning of their falsity. I was much interested in listening to a friend's description of pearl fishing, and he told me how many were worthless, and had to be thrown away which had been brought from the deep in good faith. I thought it was so with mothers. All these things told to their children, is in a firm belief, that they are doing the child no harm; while the true pearl of truth is lying near them, they prefer a false one which will embitter their future. Oftentimes have I been pained to hear mothers tell their children about "Blue Bear[d] who killed and ate children;" and those dear children will remember those things, long after the mother has gone to rest, and remember the horror they felt whenever they were alone, after dark, for fear they were to furnish meat for Blue Beard's dinner. Life is far too short to be darkened by such untruths, and their effects, and there are so many true, beautiful and useful pearls, to give children. All nature is open to the mother, and she can call truths suited to her children's understanding, and she has God's own book filled with inspired wisdom, and while her own heart is filled with its teachings, she may teach the children to find the true pearl, the "Pearl of great price."[3] Mothers talk to your little ones for eternity.

—Semper Fidelis

1. From "The Clock Is on the Stroke of Six" by Mary Howitt (1799–1888).
2. A reference to the devil.
3. Drawn from Matthew 13:45–46, which reads "Again, the kingdom of heaven is like unto a merchant man, seeking goodly pearls, who, when he had found one pearl of great price, went and sold all that he had, and bought it."

Appendix B

Issues of the *Elevator* Consulted

All of the following issues have been located by the California Newspaper Project. Strong evidence suggests that at least some of the missing issues from 1867 to 1877 included work by Carter. It also seems likely that the *Elevator* would have noticed her death in August of 1881. All of the issues below have also been microfilmed and can be viewed at most major research university libraries.

The editor of this volume would appreciate corresponding with individuals who hold copies of issues not included on the list below.

Issues consulted:
7 April 1865–30 March 1866
26 October 1866
11 January 1867
21 June 1867
5 July 1867
16 August 1867–2 July 1869
16 July 1869
30 July 1869
18 August 1869–3 September 1869
17 September 1869
15 October 1869
29 October 1869–3 December 1869
17 December 1869–31 December 1869
11 February 1870–25 February 1870
11 March 1870–25 March 1870
15 April 1870
22 April 1870
6 May 1870

27 May 1870–8 July 1870
2 December 1870
18 October 1871
29 December 1871
27 April 1872–22 June 1872
20 July 1872–3 August 1872
24 August 1872
31 August 1872
14 September 1872
21 September 1872
5 October 1872
18 October 1872–5 July 1873
19 July 1873–27 December 1873
10 January 1874–7 February 1874
21 February 1874–16 May 1874
30 May 1874–26 December 1874
28 August 1875
17 March 1877
31 March 1877
7 April 1877
3 December 1881
2 May 1885
3 July 1886
11 September 1886
11 October 1890
18 October 1890
18 June 1892
11 June 1898

Works Cited

NEWSPAPERS

Christian Recorder (Philadelphia, Pennsylvania).
Colored American (New York City, New York).
Elevator (San Francisco, California).
Frederick Douglass's Paper (Rochester, New York).
Liberator (Boston, Massachusetts).
Nevada Daily Transcript (Nevada City, California).
North Star (Rochester, New York).
Pacific Appeal (San Francisco, California).
Plaindealer (Detroit, Michigan).
San Francisco Bulletin (San Francisco, California).

VITAL RECORDS AND GOVERNMENT DOCUMENTS

1840, 1850, 1860, 1870, 1880, 1900 Federal Censuses.
1847 Quaker Census of Philadelphia African Americans. Available online at http://www.swarthmore.edu/library/friends/paac1847/main.html.
Nevada County, California Marriage Records.

BOOKS, ARTICLES, DISSERTATIONS, AND PAPERS

Abijian, James de T., comp. *Blacks and Their Contributions to the American West: A Bibliography and Union List of Library Holdings through 1970*. Boston: G. K. Hall, 1974.
Allmendinger, Blake. *Imagining the African American West*. Lincoln: University of Nebraska Press, 2005.

American Newspaper Directory. New York: George P. Rowell and Company, 1869.

Anderson, Gayle. "The Public Career of Edward Dickinson Baker." PhD diss., Vanderbilt University, 1960.

Beasley, Delilah L. *Negro Trail Blazers of California*. Los Angeles: Times Mirror, 1919.

Beckwourth, James P. *The Life and Adventures of James P. Beckwourth*. Edited by Delmont R. Oswald. Lincoln: University of Nebraska Press, 1972.

Berlin, Ira. *Slaves without Masters: The Free Negro in the Antebellum South*. New York: New Press, 1974.

Black Americans in Congress, 1870–1989. Washington, D.C.: Government Printing Office, 1991.

Boyd, Melba Joyce. *Discarded Legacy: Politics and Poetics in the Life of Frances E. W. Harper, 1825–1911*. Detroit: Wayne State University Press, 1994.

Brink, Carol. *Harps in the Wind*. New York: Macmillan, 1947.

Bronson, Orval. *Nevada City*. Nevada City, CA: Nevada County Historical Society, 2002.

Broussard, Albert S. *Black San Francisco: The Struggle for Racial Equality in the West, 1900–1954*. Lawrence: University of Kansas Press, 1993.

Bullock, Penelope. *The Afro-American Periodical Press, 1838–1909*. Baton Rouge: Louisiana State University Press, 1981.

Burt, Olive. *Negroes in the Early West*. New York: Messner, 1969.

Collins, Julia. *The Curse of Caste*. Edited by Mitch Kachun and William Andrews. New York: Oxford University Press, 2006.

Crane, Lauren E., ed. *Newton Booth of California: His Speeches and Addresses*. New York: G. P. Putnam's Sons, 1894.

Cranon, William. *Nature's Metropolis*. New York: W. W. Norton, 1992.

Daniels, Douglas Henry. *Pioneer Urbanites: A Social and Cultural History of Black San Francisco*. Berkeley: University of California Press, 1990.

Dayton, Frederick Erving. *Steamboat Days*. New York: Stokes, 1875.

de Graaf, Lawrence B., Kevin Malroy, and Quintard Taylor, eds. *Seeking El Dorado: sAfrican Americans in California*. Seattle: University of Seattle Press, 2001.

Delany, Martin. *Blake, or the Huts of America*. Boston: Beacon, 1970.

Demartus, DeEtta. *The Force of a Feather: The Search for a Lost Story of Slavery and Freedom*. Salt Lake City: University of Utah Press, 2002.

Detter, Thomas. *Nellie Brown, or the Jealous Wife, with Other Sketches*. Edited by Frances Smith Foster. Lincoln: University of Nebraska Press, 1996.

Donald, David Herbert. *Charles Sumner*. New York: DeCapo, 1996.

DuBois, Ellen Carol. *Feminism and Suffrage*. Ithaca: Cornell University Press, 1999.

Etulian, Robert W., and N. Jill Howard. *A Bibliographical Guide to the Study of Western American Literature*. 2nd ed. Albuquerque: University of New Mexico Press, 1995.

Finkelman, Paul. "The Law of Slavery and Freedom in California, 1848–1860." *California Western Law Review* 17 (1981): 437–464.

Flipper, Henry Ossian. *The Colored Cadet at West Point*. Edited by Quintard Taylor. Lincoln: University of Nebraska Press, 1998.

Foster, Frances Smith. "A Narrative of the Interesting Origins and (Somewhat) Surprising Developments of African-American Print Culture." *American Literary History* 17 no. 4 (Winter 2005): 714–740.

———. *Written by Herself: Literary Production by African American Women, 1746–1892.* Bloomington: Indiana University Press, 1993.

Gara, Larry. *The Liberty Line.* Lexington: University of Kentucky Press, 1996.

———. "William Still." In *African American Lives,* edited by Henry Louis Gates, Jr., and Evelyn Brooks Higginbotham, 790–791. New York: Oxford University Press, 2004.

Gardner, Eric. "African American Women's Poetry in the *Christian Recorder,* 1855–1865: A Bio-Bibliography with Sample Poems." *African American Review* 40 no. 4: 813–831.

———. "Amelia E. Johnson." In *African American National Biography,* edited by Henry Louis Gates, Jr., and Evelyn Brooks Higginbotham, forthcoming in 2008.

———. "Elizabeth Taylor Greenfield." In *African American Lives,* edited by Henry Louis Gates, Jr., and Evelyn Brooks Higginbotham, 352–354. New York: Oxford University Press, 2004.

———. "Mifflin Wistar Gibbs." In *African American National Biography,* edited by Henry Louis Gates, Jr., and Evelyn Brooks Higginbotham, forthcoming in 2008.

———. "Thomas Detter." In *African American National Biography,* edited by Henry Louis Gates, Jr., and Evelyn Brooks Higginbotham, forthcoming in 2008.

———, ed. "Two 'New' Texts from the Pen of Mrs. Maria W. Stewart." *PMLA,* forthcoming.

Gensler, Andy. "Frank Johnson." In *African American Lives,* edited by Henry Louis Gates, Jr., and Evelyn Brooks Higginbotham, 452–454. New York: Oxford University Press, 2004.

Gibbs, Mifflin Wistar. *Shadow and Light.* Edited by Tom W. Dillard. Lincoln: University of Nebraska Press, 1995.

Giddings, Paula. *When and Where I Enter: The Impact of Black Women on Race and Sex in America.* New York: William Morrow and Company, 1984.

Glasrud, Bruce A., comp. *African Americans in the West: A Bibliography of Secondary Sources.* Alpine, TX: Sul Ross State University Press, 1998.

Glasrud, Bruce, and Laurie Champion, eds. *The African American West: A Century of Stories.* Boulder: University Press of Colorado, 2000.

Goodyear, Frank H. "'Beneath the Shadow of Her Flag': Philip A. Bell's *The Elevator* and the Struggle for Enfranchisement." *California History* 78 no. 1 (1999): 26–39 and 71–73.

Gorham, George C. "Autobiography and Reminiscence of George C. Gorham." Manuscript available through the Online Archive of California, http://www.oac.cdlib.org.

Handy, James A. *Scraps of African Methodist Episcopal History.* Philadelphia: A.M.E. Book Concern, 1902.

Harper, Frances Ellen Watkins. *Minnie's Sacrifice, Sowing and Reaping, Trial and Triumph.* Edited by Frances Smith Foster. Boston: Beacon Press, 1994.

Harris, Leslie M. *In the Shadow of Slavery: African Americans in New York City, 1626–1863.* Chicago: University of Chicago Press, 2004.

Heap, Gwinn Harrir. *Central Route to the Pacific.* Philadelphia: Lippincott, Grambo, 1854.

Hill, Daniel G. *The Freedom Seekers: Blacks in Early Canada.* Toronto: Book Society of Canada, 1981.

Hopkins, Pauline. *Winona.* In *The Magazine Novels of Pauline Hopkins.* New York: Oxford University Press, 1988.

Hudson, Lynn M. *The Making of "Mammy Pleasant": A Black Entrepreneur in Nineteenth-Century San Francisco.* Urbana: University of Illinois Press, 2003.

Hughes, Langston. *Langston Hughes and the Chicago Defender: Essays on Race, Politics, and Culture, 1942–1962.* Edited by Christopher DeSatis. Urbana: University of Illinois Press, 1995.

Hunter, Tera. *To 'Joy My Freedom: Southern Black Women's Lives and Labors after the Civil War.* Cambridge: Harvard University Press, 1997.

In Memorial [to Joseph Augustine Benton]. San Francisco: Trustees of Pacific Theological Seminary, 1892.

Jackson, Cassandra. "Frances Ellen Watkins Harper." In *African American Lives*, edited by Henry Louis Gates, Jr., and Evelyn Brooks Higginbotham, 374–376. New York: Oxford University Press, 2004.

Johnson, Michael K. *Black Masculinity and the Frontier Myth in American Literature.* Norman: University of Oklahoma Press, 2002.

Johnson, Susie Warren. "The Joynes Family of Accomack and Northampton Counties, Virginia." *William and Mary Quarterly* 18 no. 4 (October 1938): 499–505.

Jones, Pat. "Nevada County's Black Pioneers." *Nevada County Historical Bulletin* 39 no. 3 (July 1985): 19–24.

Joynes, Levin S. *A Sketch of the Life of Thomas Joynes.* Columbia, SC: R. L. Bryan Co., 1876.

Kachun, Mitch. *Festivals of Freedom: Memory and Meaning in African American Emancipation Celebrations, 1808–1915.* Amherst: University of Massachusetts Press, 2003.

Katz, William Loren. *The Black West.* Rev. ed. New York: Harlem Moon/Broadway, 2005.

Kelly, Howard A. *Dictionary of American Medical Biography.* New York: D. Appleton, 1928.

Klingman, Peter D. *Josiah Walls.* Gainesville: University of Florida Press, 1976.

Kowalewski, Michael, ed. *Reading the West: New Essays on the Literature of the American West.* Cambridge: Cambridge University Press, 1996.

Lape, Noreen Groover. *West of the Border: The Multicultural Literature of the Western American Frontiers.* Athens, OH: Ohio University Press, 2000.

Lapp, Rudolph M. *Afro-Americans in California.* 2nd ed. San Francisco: Boyd and Fraser, 1987.

———. *Blacks in Gold Rush California.* New Haven: Yale University Press, 1977.

Lapp, Rudolph M., and Robert J. Chandler, "The Antiracism of Thomas Starr King," *Southern California Quarterly* 82 no. 4 (2000): 323–342.

Levine, Robert S. "'I, Too, Sing America': James M. Whitfield's *American and Other Poems.*" Available at http://www.classroomelectric.org/volume1/levine/intro.html.

Levy, Jo Ann. *They Saw the Elephant: Women in the California Gold Rush.* Norman: University of Oklahoma Press, 1992.

Lewis, Nathaniel. *Unsettling the Literary West: Authenticity and Authorship.* Lincoln: University of Nebraska Press, 2003.

Love, Nat. *The Life and Adventures of Nat Love.* Edited by Brackette F. Williams. Lincoln: University of Nebraska Press, 1995.

Lyons, Greg, ed. *Literature of the American West: A Cultural Approach.* New York: Longman, 2003.

[Mackey, Albert Gallatin]. *The Political Treason of Senator F. A. Sawyer and Representative C. C. Bowen*. Charleston, SC: np, 1869.

Mann, Ralph. *After the Gold Rush: Society in Grass Valley and Nevada City, California 1849–1870*. Stanford: Stanford University Press, 1982.

McHenry, Elizabeth. *Forgotten Readers: Recovering the Lost History of African American Literary Societies*. Durham: Duke University Press, 2002.

Mead, Rebecca J. *How the Vote Was Won: Women's Suffrage in the Western U.S., 1868–1914*. New York: New York University Press, 2004.

Memorial and Biographical History of Northern California. San Francisco: Lewis, 1891.

Montesano, Philip. "Philip Alexander Bell." In *African American Lives*, edited by Henry Louis Gates, Jr., and Evelyn Brooks Higginbotham, 69–71. New York: Oxford University Press, 2004.

———. "San Francisco Black Churches in the Early 1860s." *California Historical Quarterly* 52 no. 2 (1973): 145–152.

Moody, Joycelyn. *Sentimental Confessions: Spiritual Narratives of Nineteenth-Century African American Women*. Athens, GA: University of Georgia Press, 2001.

Moore, Shirley Ann Wilson. "'We Feel the Want of Protection': The Politics of Law and Race in California, 1848–1878." *California History* 81 no. 3–4 (2003): 96–125.

———. "African Americans in California: A Brief Historiography." *California History* 75 no. 3 (1996): 214–222.

Moos, Dan. *Outside America: Race, Ethnicity, and the Role of the American West in National Belonging*. Hanover, NH: Dartmouth College Press, 2005.

Mungen, Donna. *The Life and Times of Biddy Mason*. Los Angeles: MC Printing, 1976.

Nankivell, John H. *Buffalo Soldier Regiment*. Edited by Quintard Taylor. Lincoln: University of Nebraska Press, 2001.

Okker, Patricia. *Our Sister Editors: Sarah J. Hale and the Tradition of Nineteenth-Century American Women Editors*. Athens, GA: University of Georgia Press, 1995.

Peterson, Carla. *"Doers of the Word": African American Women Speakers and Writers in the North (1830–1880)*. New York: Oxford University Press, 1995.

Randall, Ruth Painter. *Colonel Elmer Ellsworth*. Boston: Little, Brown, 1960.

Reynolds, David S. *John Brown, Abolitionist*. New York: Knopf, 2005.

Rice, Richard B., William A. Bullough, and Richard J. Orsi. *The Elusive Eden*. 2nd ed. Boston: McGraw-Hill, 1996.

Richardson, Marilyn, ed. *Maria W. Stewart, America's First Black Woman Political Writer*. Bloomington: Indiana University Press, 1987.

Ridout, Lionel Utley. "The Church, the Chinese, and the Negroes in California." *Historical Magazine of the Protestant Episcopal Church* 28 (June 1959): 115–138.

Rivo, Lisa E. "Edmonia Lewis." In *African American Lives*, edited by Henry Louis Gates, Jr., and Evelyn Brooks Higginbotham, 529–531. New York: Oxford University Press, 2004.

Robinson, Marcia C. "Frances Watkins Harper: Black Abolitionist among the Women of Maine, 1854–1856." Colloquium, Library Company of Philadelphia, 26 May 2006.

Romero, Lora. *Home Fronts: Domesticity and Its Critics in the Antebellum United States*. Durham: Duke University Press, 1997.

Rooks, Noliwe. *Ladies' Pages: African American Women's Magazines and the Culture That Made Them*. New Brunswick: Rutgers University Press, 2004.

Rusco, Elmer. *Good Time Coming? Black Nevadans.* Westport, CT: Greenwood, 1976.

———. "Thomas Detter: Nevada Black Writer and Advocate for Human Rights." *Nevada Historical Society Quarterly* 47 no. 3 (2004): 193–213.

Sanda [Walter Stowers and William Anderson]. *Appointed: An American Novel.* Detroit: Detroit Law Printing Company, 1894.

Shankman, Arnold. "Black on Yellow: Afro-Americans View Chinese-Americans, 1850–1935." *Phylon* 39 no. 1 (1978): 1–17.

Sherman, Joan R. *Invisible Poets: Afro-Americans in the Nineteenth Century.* Rev. ed. Urbana: University of Illinois Press, 1989.

Snorgrass, J. William. "The Black Press in the San Francisco Bay Area, 1856–1900." *California History* 60 no. 4 (1981–1982): 306–317.

Stanley, Gerald. "Frank Pixley and the Heathen Chinese." *Phylon* 40 no. 3 (1979): 224–228.

Stewart, James Brewer. *Wendell Phillips: Liberty's Hero.* Baton Rouge: Louisiana State University Press, 1998.

Taylor, John M. *William Henry Seward.* New York: HarperCollins, 1991.

Taylor, Quintard. *In Search of the Racial Frontier: African Americans in the American West, 1528–1990.* New York: W. W. Norton, 1998.

Taylor, Quintard, and Shirley Ann Wilson Moore, eds. *African American Women Confront the West, 1600–1900.* Norman: University of Oklahoma Press, 2003.

Thornton, Willis. *The Nine Lives of Citizen Train.* New York: Greenberg, 1948.

Turner, Glennette Tilley. *The Underground Railroad in Illinois.* Wheaton, IL: Newman, 2001.

Ware, W. Porter, and Thaddeus C. Lockard, Jr. *P. T. Barnum Presents Jenny Lind.* Baton Rouge: Louisiana State University Press, 1980.

Welke, Barbara Y. "Rights of Passage: Gendered-Rights Consciousness and the Quest for Freedom, San Francisco, California, 1850–1870." In *African American Women Confront the West 1600–1900,* edited by Quintard Taylor and Shirley Ann Wilson Moore, 73–96. Norman: University of Oklahoma Press, 2003.

Wells, Harry Laurenz. *History of Nevada County, California.* Oakland: Thompson and Wells, 1880.

Whitfield, James Monroe. *America and Other Poems.* Buffalo: James S. Leavitt, 1853.

Wilder, Theodore. *History of Company C of the 7th Regiment of Ohio Volunteer Infantry.* Oberlin, OH: J.B.T., 1866.

Williams, James. *The Life and Adventures of James Williams.* Edited by Malcolm J. Rohrbough. Lincoln: University of Nebraska Press, 2002.

Williams, Robert C. *Horace Greeley: Champion of American Freedom.* New York: New York University, 2006.

Wilson, Lawrence. *Itinerary of the 7th Ohio Volunteer Infantry.* New York: Neale Publishing 1907.

Young, James L. *Helen Duval: A French Romance.* San Francisco: The Bancroft Company, 1891.

Index

CPSIA information can be obtained
at www.ICGtesting.com
Printed in the USA
FSHW012001070421
80277FS